D1196132

WITHDRAWN
No longer the property of the
Boston Public Library.
Sale of this material benefits the Library

THE IMPORTANCE OF

Thomas Jefferson

by
Don Nardo

Lucent Books, P.O. Box 289011, San Diego, CA 92198-9011

These and other titles are included in The Importance Of
biography series:

Benjamin Franklin
Thomas Jefferson
Chief Joseph
Christopher Columbus
Marie Curie
Galileo Galilei
Michelangelo
Wolfgang Amadeus Mozart
Richard M. Nixon
Jackie Robinson
Margaret Sanger
H.G. Wells

Thomas Jefferson

Dudley Branch Library
65 Warren Street
Roxbury, MA 02119-3206

23

Library of Congress Cataloging-in-Publication Data

Nardo, Don, 1947–
    Thomas Jefferson / by Don Nardo.
        p.   cm. — (The Importance of)
    Includes bibliographical references and index.
    Summary: A biography of Thomas Jefferson from his youth to his presidency, his role as a diplomat, and his enduring legacy.
    ISBN 1-56006-037-9
    1. Jefferson, Thomas, 1743–1826—Juvenile literature.
    2. Presidents—United States—Biography—Juvenile literature.
    [1. Jefferson, Thomas, 1743–1826. 2. Presidents.]. I. Title.
    II. Series.
    E332.79.N37   1993
    973.4'6'092—dc20
    [B]   92-43913
                                                        CIP
                                                         AC

YA

7/93

Copyright 1993 by Lucent Books, Inc., P.O. Box 289011, San Diego, California, 92198-9011

No part of this book may be reproduced or used in any other form or by any other means, electrical, mechanical, or otherwise, including, but not limited to, photocopy, recording, or any information storage and retrieval system, without prior written permission from the publisher.

Contents

Foreword

THE IMPORTANCE OF biography series deals with individuals who have made a unique contribution to history. The editors of the series have deliberately chosen to cast a wide net and include people from all fields of endeavor. Individuals from politics, music, art, literature, philosophy, science, sports, and religion are all represented. In addition, the editors did not restrict the series to individuals whose accomplishments have helped change the course of history. Of necessity, this criterion would have eliminated many whose contribution was great, though limited. Charles Darwin, for example, was responsible for radically altering the scientific view of the natural history of the world. His achievements continue to impact the study of science today. Others, such as Chief Joseph of the Nez Percé, played a pivotal role in the history of their own people. While Joseph's influence does not extend much beyond the Nez Percé, his nonviolent resistance to white expansion and his continuing role in protecting his tribe and his homeland remain an inspiration to all.

These biographies are more than factual chronicles. Each volume attempts to emphasize an individual's contributions both in his or her own time and for posterity. For example, the voyages of Christopher Columbus opened the way to European colonization of the New World. Unquestionably, his encounter with the New World brought monumental changes to both Europe and the Americas in his day. Today, however, the broader impact of Columbus's voyages is being critically scrutinized. *Christopher Columbus,* as well as every biography in The Importance Of series, includes and evaluates the most recent scholarship available on each subject.

Each author includes a wide variety of primary and secondary source quotations to document and substantiate his or her work. All quotes are footnoted to show readers exactly how and where biographers derive their information, as well as provide stepping stones to further research. These quotations enliven the text by giving readers eyewitness views of the life and times of each individual covered in The Importance Of series.

Finally, each volume is enhanced by photographs, bibliographies, chronologies, and comprehensive indexes. For both the casual reader and the student engaged in research, The Importance Of biographies will be a fascinating adventure into the lives of people who have helped shape humanity's past, present, and will continue to shape its future.

Important Dates in the Life of Thomas Jefferson

Jefferson is born at Shadwell, — **1743**
his father's Virginia
plantation.

1760 — Attends College of William
and Mary in Williamsburg,
Elected to Virginia's — **1768** Virginia.
House of Burgesses.
1772 — Marries Martha
Writes *A Summary View of the* — **1774** Wayles Skelton.
Rights of British America.
1776 — Writes the Declaration
of Independence.
Appointed Governor — **1779**
of Virginia.

1785-
1789 }— Serves as minister to France.

Becomes first U.S. — **1790**
secretary of state.
1796 — Elected vice-president
of the United States.

Elected third president — **1801**
of the United States.
1803 — Purchases Louisiana territory
from France for fifteen
Elected to second term — **1804** million dollars, nearly
as president. doubling the size of the
1809 United States.
Retires to Monticello.

1816-
1819 }— Helps found the
University of Virginia.

Dies at Monticello. — **1826**

A Mind That Asked "Why?"

In 1962, President John F. Kennedy greeted a group of Nobel Prize–winning scientists, writers, and thinkers at the White House. They represented many disciplines, from chemistry and physics to literature and phi-

Thomas Jefferson was an extraordinary man. His interests and achievements spanned the fields of politics, science, literature, and architecture.

losophy. With a grin, Kennedy called them "the most extraordinary collection of talents . . . that has ever gathered together at the White House, with the possible exception of when Thomas Jefferson dined alone."[1]

Kennedy's quip acknowledged that Thomas Jefferson was more than one of the country's Founding Fathers. Jefferson's most often cited achievements—his authorship of the Declaration of Independence and his service as the country's third president—would be enough to ensure any person an honored place in history. But Jefferson was much more than a patriot and politician. "Statesman, diplomat, author, scientist, architect . . . political theorist, inventor—Jefferson was all of these," remarked biographer Roger Bruns. "He was, in an age of many great men, one of the most extraordinary."[2]

Jefferson's numerous achievements ranged from founding and designing the University of Virginia to devising the monetary system still used in the United States. His interests and activities were incredibly diverse. He regularly observed the stars and planets. He also compiled a scholarly volume listing the known animals and plants of his native state of Virginia, and he experimented with growing

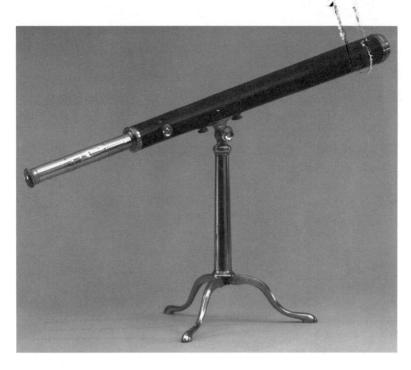

With this telescope, at his Monticello home, Jefferson gazed at the comets, stars, and planets and pondered their ever-changing positions.

wine grapes. In addition, he invented the dumbwaiter, a new kind of plow, and other useful devices. These were but a few of his accomplishments.

The driving force behind Jefferson's wide-ranging interests and achievements was his constantly inquiring mind. He looked out upon the world and wondered why things appeared or worked the way they did. "Nothing was so ordinary or taken-for-granted that it could escape his scrutiny and his questioning," wrote author Johanna Johnston. "And because he was extraordinarily talented in dozens of different ways—one of the most versatile geniuses who ever lived—this tireless interest in everything led him to accomplish surprising things."[3]

With such a questioning mind, it is no wonder, then, that Jefferson reexamined the traditional ways people governed themselves. He saw that the system in his own society had flaws, and he envisioned a better one. And it is for his contributions to the creation of the U.S. government that he achieved immortality.

But aside from his deeds, this remarkable man left behind another kind of legacy: an example for future generations of how to view, question, and improve the world. Jefferson tried to see, appreciate, and analyze all the works of nature and humanity. After thorough observation and examination, he demonstrated that the next logical step is to make things better.

1 A Thirst for Knowledge

On the thirteenth day of April in 1743, Peter Jefferson nervously paced his well-furnished parlor. Through the window, he could see the fields of Shadwell, the thousand-acre plantation he had built six years before on the banks of the Rivanna River in the British colony of Virginia. Every few minutes, the man glanced at the antique clock that rested between two pieces of fine Venetian glassware on the mantle. He also periodically looked toward the house's rear bedroom, from which he could occasionally hear feverish moans. He found that he was just as nervous waiting for his third child to be born as he had been for the first two.

Suddenly, a loud cry from the back bedroom interrupted his musings. Peter Jefferson ran down the corridor and waited outside the delivery room until the doctor emerged a few seconds later. "A boy, Mr. Jefferson," said the doctor. "A boy. Weighs nine pounds, I'll warrant, and wonderfully strong." A few minutes later, one of Jefferson's female slaves appeared carrying the child, whom Peter and his wife, Jane, had decided to name Thomas. The slave woman remarked on the baby's prominent shock of red hair as the father carefully took him in his arms. "He looks worried," said Peter Jefferson with a smile.[4]

A Fascination for Nature

Young Thomas Jefferson's look of worry quickly gave way to one of wonder and fascination. From the beginning, his parents noted that he was unusually alert, bright, and interested in everything around him. The boy questioned how things worked. He asked about what lay at the end of a road or beyond the next stream or meadow. He was especially interested in learning the secrets of the forests and mountains that stretched from the western boundary of Shadwell toward the distant horizon. Biographer Leonard Wibberley describes what this part of the country was like when Peter Jefferson built Shadwell:

There were only two or three other settlers in the area. Virgin forest covered the land and there were but a few trails through it and those uncertain. People traveled on foot or on horseback and had often to dismount and hack their way through thickets. The area was known as the Piedmont country, meaning, "the country at the foot of the mountains." Westward the land rose in a series of mountain chains dominated by the Blue Ridge Mountains. They were forest-clad mountains thickly covered

Jefferson's mill at his Shadwell plantation. As a boy, Jefferson spent many hours exploring the dense forests and mountains near Shadwell.

with magnificent growths of oak, beech, elm, and pine. The true frontier with its stockades and blockhouses lay only a hundred miles west of Shadwell. . . . On this plantation there was a little mountain. . . . When Tom Jefferson was old enough his father often took him to the top . . . to see the view. . . .

"What lies beyond the mountains?" he asked his father.

"More mountains."

"And beyond them?"

"A big river—the Mississippi."

"And beyond the river?"

Peter Jefferson shrugged. "Nobody knows for sure."[5]

The desire to know what lay beyond the horizon became a lifelong interest for Thomas Jefferson.

It was not only the land itself but also what lived on the land that fascinated Jefferson. From the time he could walk and talk, he was keenly interested in all of the natural life around him. He spent hours observing the birds, forest animals, insects, flowers, and trees of the Piedmont region. His father encouraged the boy's curiosity and desire to learn. Although Peter Jefferson had little formal education, he did have a questioning mind and an interest in the wonders of nature. The elder Jefferson taught his young son to carry notebooks everywhere and keep records of his observations. Even at the age of ten, the boy kept unusually detailed and thorough records. In the dozens of notebooks he kept as a child, he did more than just list what he saw. He recorded the sizes, textures, and colors of the animals and trees. He noted the animals' habitats and activities and described the changes in vegetation and animal populations over the course of the seasons.

A Site for Monticello

One of Jefferson's greatest childhood joys was hiking through the woods and hills of Virginia's rural Piedmont area. On one of these nature walks when he was thirteen, Jefferson and a school friend named Dabney Carr came upon the hilltop on which Jefferson would one day build his famous home—Monticello. In her book Thomas Jefferson: His Many Talents, *Johanna Johnston describes the scene:*

"Then, one day, as they were wandering on one of the hills that lay across the Rivanna [the river near the Jefferson plantation], they made a wonderful discovery. They had climbed a long, rough way through the virgin forest, and at last they came out on the top of the hill. And both of them stopped and stared. It was not the highest hill anywhere about, but somehow from this hilltop they had a view like none they had seen before. The whole world seemed spread out below them, hills and valleys rolling endlessly to the horizon both east and west. They were silent a moment looking. Then . . . young Dabney . . . told Thomas that here, on this hilltop, was where he wanted to be buried when he died. Solemnly, Thomas nodded in agreement. He wanted to be buried there, too. Then Thomas had a less sombre thought. This was more than a place to be buried. This was a spot on which to live. 'This is where I am going to build my house one day,' he said. Dabney looked at him. 'A house—here? On a hilltop?' Nobody built houses on hilltops. Houses were built in the lowlands, by rivers or streams, so that crops . . . would have easy transport to the coast. But 'Why not?' asked Thomas. . . . Why should he not build on a hilltop? There would be ways to solve the problems. He would figure out ways. Because, as he stared out over the rolling hills, he felt sure that no one could ever be or think anything mean or small up here. Every thought must surely be tempered by this great vista into goodness and beauty. 'Yes, this is where I will build my house,' said Thomas."

Dabney Carr died suddenly in May 1773. Remembering Carr's childhood wish, Jefferson had him buried on the beautiful hilltop near Jefferson's new home. Beside the grave, Jefferson placed a stone, on which he carved: "Dabney Carr: To his Virtue, Good Sense, Learning and Friendship, this stone is dedicated by Thomas Jefferson, who of all men living loved him most."

Rejecting Class Distinctions

In addition to the plants and animals of the countryside, young Thomas Jefferson closely observed the people around him and their habits, customs, and activities. Much of what he learned about the world and his own society came from his father. Peter Jefferson introduced his son to the polite ways of what he and many others called the Virginia aristocracy. This was the class of well-to-do landowners whose large holdings of money, land, and slaves made them very influential and powerful. The landed aristocracy also controlled the House of Burgesses, which was the colony's governing body located in Williamsburg, Virginia. Answering to King George III and the British government, the House considered and enacted local laws that affected the colony. In a letter to a friend,

The landed aristocracy of Virginia lived in wealth and splendor. This is the life into which Jefferson was born.

For all its power and influence, Virginia's governing body, the House of Burgesses, still answered to King George III of Great Britain.

the adult Thomas Jefferson described the Virginia aristocracy he remembered from his boyhood:

> Certain families had risen to splendor by wealth and the preservation of it from generation to generation . . . some had produced a series of men of talents; families in general had remained stationary on the grounds of their forefathers, for there was no emigration to the westward in those days.[6]

The life-style of the colonial aristocrats was often colorful and romantic. This was especially true of the young men, who were very concerned with appearing adventurous and dashing. They also tried to keep up with the latest fashions and manners popular in European courts. According to author and historian Vincent Sheean,

> The art of flourishing a plumed hat and making a court bow was encouraged as much at Williamsburg as in London. No Virginia gentleman went to an evening party without either a powdered wig or a thorough job of powdering his own hair.[7]

Although Peter Jefferson had not been born into this aristocratic class, he had married into it. Jane Jefferson was a member of the Randolph family, one of the richest and most powerful in Virginia. Thanks to gifts of land by the Randolphs, Shadwell became a prosperous plantation producing plentiful crops of tobacco, Virginia's chief cash crop.

Born into this prosperity, young Thomas Jefferson quickly learned the manners and customs of the landed class. He saw that most members regarded themselves as superior to the small farmers of the countryside as well as to the merchants and laborers of the cities. But even as a child, Jefferson was uncomfortable with such distinctions. His sharp powers of observation told him that the well-to-do were no more intelligent than others. Nor were the aristocrats more hard-working or God-fearing than those they looked down upon. Jefferson came to view the idea of class distinctions as groundless and silly, and he rejected the idea that he was better than anyone else simply because of his money and family. He later criticized what he called "an artificial aristocracy founded on wealth and birth, without either virtue or talents." By contrast, he said, "there is a natural aristocracy among men. The grounds of this are virtue and talents. . . . The natural aristocracy I consider as the most precious gift of nature for the instruction, the trusts, and government of society."[8]

The colonial aristocracy lived in a world much like that of the wealthy classes in Britain. At parties, women wore fashionable plumed hats and men donned powdered wigs.

Varied Avenues of Learning

By deed rather than by word, Peter Jefferson regularly reinforced his son's observations about the inherent worth of all people. Peter Jefferson treated the family's slaves in a kindly manner. Most slave owners treated their slaves like animals, often beating and sometimes even killing them. Although Peter Jefferson did not consider slaves equal to whites, he did see them as human and therefore treated them more humanely than most of his neighbors did. Young Thomas Jefferson believed that slavery was wrong. But when he eventually inherited the plantation, Jefferson did not free his slaves because he was sincerely worried that they would not be able to

At a young age Jefferson came to believe that slavery was wrong. But he did not free his slaves when he inherited Shadwell.

Negroes for Sale.

A Cargo of very fine stout Men and Women, in good order and fit for immediate service, just imported from the Windward Coast of Africa, in the Ship Two Brothers.— Conditions are one half Cash or Produce, the other half payable the first of January next, giving Bond and Security if required.

The Sale to be opened at 10 o'Clock each Day, in Mr. Bourdeaux's Yard, at No. 48, on the Bay. May 19, 1784.   JOHN MITCHELL.

Thirty Seasoned Negroes

To be Sold for Credit, at Private Sale.

AMONGST which is a Carpenter, none of whom are known to be dishonest.

Also to be sold for Cash, a regular bred young Negroe Man-Cook, born in this Country, who served several Years under an exceeding good French Cook abroad, and his Wife a middle aged Washer-Woman, (both very honest) and their two Children.—Likewise a young Man a Carpenter.

For Terms apply to the Printer.

Many slaves were brutally beaten by their owners. Although Jefferson's father did not consider black slaves his equals, he treated them more humanely than did many of his neighbors.

fend for themselves. "As far as I can judge from the experiments which have been made," he wrote to a friend, "to give liberty to, or rather, to abandon persons whose habits have been formed in slavery is like abandoning children."[9]

Black slaves were not the only deprived group that Peter Jefferson treated with respect. The elder Jefferson, who had done some exploring and surveying of Indian lands, had acquired a number of Indian

Colonial Americans often treated native Americans with the same disrespect they showed blacks. Here, colonists burn an Indian village.

friends. Although most other whites considered the Indians to be inferior savages, it was not uncommon for a hundred Cherokees at a time to visit Shadwell and camp near the Jefferson house. As a result, the young Jefferson gained sympathy and respect for the two groups white society looked down on the most—the slaves and the Indians.

Formal Education

In 1748, when Thomas Jefferson was five, his parents hired a tutor to teach him and his two older sisters, Jane and Mary, mathematics, reading, and writing. Peter and

Schoolhouse at Tuckahoe, where young Thomas Jefferson attended school. One of his least favorite subjects was Latin.

Jane Jefferson were both emphatic about giving their children the best formal education possible. At nine, young Jefferson entered a school in a neighboring county, where he studied the classics, including Latin. At the time, these subjects were considered the most essential for young men of the upper class to know. At first, the boy found learning so many unfamiliar foreign words a drudgery. But later, Jefferson very much appreciated having learned the classics. "To read the Latin and Greek authors in their original is a sublime luxury," he said years later. "I thank on my knees him who directed my early education for having put into my possession this rich source of delight; and I would not exchange it for anything which I could have then acquired, and have not since acquired."[10]

A Tremendous Loss

The man who directed Jefferson's early education, his father, died suddenly in June 1757 at the age of forty-nine. This was a tremendous loss to the boy, who had treasured Peter Jefferson's guidance and companionship. And the death changed the young man's life in many other ways. As the eldest son, he became the head of the family at the young age of fourteen. Luckily, his father had left behind a great deal of money and property. He had also put a provision in his will appointing four neighbors to manage the estate and run the plantation until the boy was older.

But Jefferson was expected to advise and make decisions for his siblings as well as take care of himself and plan his own education and future. According to friends and relatives, he did not turn to his mother,

A Family Portrait

Much of what is known about Jefferson's family and its background comes from descriptions in his adult letters and from his autobiography, published a few years after his death. In the autobiography, begun on January 6, 1821, Jefferson sketched a brief history of his family. He included one of the few written references he ever made to his mother:

"At the age of 77, I begin to make some memoranda [written records] and state some recollections of dates & facts concerning myself, for my own more ready reference & for the information of my family. The tradition in my father's family was that their ancestor came to this country from Wales, and from near the mountain of Snowdon, the highest in Gr. Br. [Great Britain]. . . . The first particular information I have of any ancestor was my grandfather who lived at the place in Chesterfield called Ozborne's. . . . He had three sons, Thomas who died young, Field who settled on the waters of Roanoke and left numerous descendents, and Peter my father, who settled on the lands I still own called Shadwell adjoining my present residence [Monticello]. He was born Feb. 29, 1707/8 and intermarried 1739 with Jane Randolph, of the age of 19, daur [daughter] of Isham Randolph one of the seven sons of that name & family [who] settled . . . [in a neighboring county]. They trace their pedigree [ancestry] far back in England & Scotland, to which let every one ascribe the faith and merit he chooses.

My father's education had been quite neglected; but being of a strong mind, sound judgment and eager after information, he read much and improved himself. . . . He died . . . [in 1757], leaving my mother a widow who lived till 1776, with 6 daurs & 2 sons, myself the elder. To my younger brother he left the estate on James river called Snowdon after the supposed birth-place of the family. To myself the lands on which I was born & live."

as he had to his father, for advice or guidance. The reason for this is unknown. In the thousands of letters he wrote in his lifetime, Jefferson mentioned his mother only twice and without affection, and their relationship remains a mystery. What is certain is that with his father gone, the boy felt alone and burdened with responsibility. Jefferson wondered at first whether he could handle the situation. He could, he knew, easily be lured into the lazy, irresponsible life-style of most young aristocrats. Jefferson described his youthful dilemma years later in a letter to a relative:

When I recollect that at fourteen years of age the whole care and direction of myself was thrown on myself entirely, without a relative or friend qualified to advise or guide me, and recollect the various sorts of bad company with which I associated from time to time, I am astonished that I did not turn off with some of them, and become as worthless to society as they were. . . . From the circumstances of my position, I was often thrown into the society of horse-racers, card-players, fox-hunters, scientific and professional men, and of dignified men; and many a time have I asked myself . . . which of these kinds of reputation should I prefer— that of a horse-jockey, a fox-hunter, an orator, or the honest advocate of my country's rights?[11]

Jefferson chose the more responsible route, proving that his father had taught him well. The young man began studying with the Reverend James Maury, an edu-cator who lived some fourteen miles from Shadwell. Maury taught Jefferson the classics as well as philosophy, history, and other subjects. He also took the boy on field trips through the Piedmont to search for fossils, collect plants, and identify and count animals. Maury recog-nized Jefferson's unusual intelligence and fueled the boy's inquiring mind and insatiable appetite for learning. For three years, Jefferson studied hard while keeping a close eye on his siblings and their problems.

Facing New Challenges

In 1760, when he was seventeen, Jefferson decided to enroll in the prestigious College of William and Mary in Williamsburg. He was still unsure of what profession to pur-sue, so he continued to study many subjects. He also found time to enjoy the crowded streets and social life of Williamsburg, which

At age seventeen Jefferson en-rolled in the prestigious Col-lege of William and Mary in Williamsburg. There, he studied many subjects and sampled the city's rich social and cultural offerings.

he found very different from life in the countryside. Roger Bruns describes the capital of Virginia at the time:

There were the buildings such as the porticoed Capitol and the magnificent governor's mansion, there were the fashionable stores, the well-to-do families riding in expensive coaches, the politicians and lawyers sporting colorful knee breeches and coats, accompanied by their ladies showing off imported dresses as they strolled along Duke of Gloucester Street. There were tradesmen, shopkeepers, craftsmen, and slaves also walking the bustling city streets. There were the acting companies to see and balls to dance at. There were the taverns, especially the Raleigh, where diners ate venison [deer], stew, and Welsh rarebit and drank punch, brandy, rum, and French wines.[12]

Jefferson found making new acquaintances in Williamsburg easy. This was partly because he was outgoing and friendly. He was also a physically imposing youth who stood out in a crowd. According to Vincent Sheean, "He was over six feet tall when he was seventeen years old—

Jefferson's Appearance

Jefferson reached physical maturity early. By the time he was ready to attend the College of William and Mary in Williamsburg, he already exhibited his distinctive and imposing, though somewhat awkward, adult stature. In his detailed study of Jefferson and his accomplishments, Thomas Jefferson and the New Nation, *Merrill D. Peterson describes what Jefferson looked like:*

"This youth of seventeen who came down from the hills to Williamsburg in 1760 had taken on the physical characteristics so commonly ascribed to him in later years. He was tall and lanky, with large hands and feet, and seemed to be growing right out of his clothes. As straight and strong as a gun-barrel, he had the sinewy [lean and muscular], broad-shouldered vigor of his father. His tousled hair was of reddish color, his eyes light and hazel, his face ruddy and freckled. His head, like his body, was spare of flesh. Lips thin and compressed suggested a mind in thought, while the angular nose and projecting chin added forcefulness to a countenance [expression] otherwise mild. He gave the appearance of the fresh country lad he was, rather more awkward than graceful, and by no stretch could he be considered handsome or polished at this stage. But he was bright, amiable, eager, and full of bounce, which more than compensated for any deficiency in looks."

a rather awkward boy, with carroty red hair and freckles, a pointed nose and chin. You would never have called him handsome, and yet his keen gray eyes and generally alert personality made him attractive to most people."[13] One acquaintance who quickly became a close friend was Doctor William Small, a mathematics professor. Small, like Jefferson's earlier teachers, recognized the boy's genius and spent many hours outside of class discussing current knowledge about science with him.

It was Small who introduced Jefferson to George Wythe, a prominent lawyer and professor. Jefferson and Wythe became friends, and in 1762, Jefferson apprenticed

While working as his apprentice, Jefferson and Wythe became close friends. Jefferson often visited Wythe's home (above).

The prominent lawyer George Wythe accepted Jefferson as his apprentice. Jefferson learned about the law by watching Wythe and others at work.

himself to Wythe as a law student. The young man did not learn the law from classes and books. Instead, as was the custom at the time, he learned from watching and doing. For five years, Jefferson ran errands for Wythe and accompanied his mentor to court. Jefferson also met other prominent lawyers and watched them work.

The Natural Rights of Citizens

Through the activities of some of these lawyers, as well as other prominent Williamsburg citizens, Jefferson witnessed the beginnings of colonial unrest against King George. One of the first signs of trouble was the verdict in a controversial 1763 court case pitting local parsons, or ministers, against Virginia's House of Burgesses.

Early Education

As an adult, Jefferson felt himself fortunate to have been influenced by several intelligent and learned men during his college days at Williamsburg. In his Autobiography, *he recalled:*

"It was my great good fortune, and what probably fixed the destinies of my life, that Dr. William Small of Scotland, was then Professor of Mathematics, a man profound in most of the useful branches of science, with a happy talent of communication, correct and gentlemanly manners, and an enlarged and liberal mind. He, most happily for me, became soon attached to me, and made me his daily companion when not engaged in school. . . . He returned to Europe in 1762, having previously filled up the measure of his goodness to me, by procuring for me, from his most intimate friend, George Wythe, a reception as a student of law, under his direction, and introduced me to the acquaintance and familiar [dining] table of Governor Fauquier, the ablest man who had ever filled that office. With him, and at his table, Dr. Small and Mr. Wythe . . . and myself, formed a *partie quaree* [party of four], and to the habitual conversations on these occasions I owed much instruction."

This became known as the Parson's Case. The House had earlier decided that the ministers, who then received salaries from the government, could no longer be paid in allotments of tobacco, which had been the custom. The ministers were to receive cash instead. Since the cash was worth less than the tobacco, the ministers objected and took their case to the king and British courts. These courts upheld the ministers' complaints. This decision angered many colonists, however, who had come to think of themselves, separated from Great Britain by thousands of miles, as largely self-governing. They felt that faraway British courts overruling Virginia lawmakers in local matters was unfair. They considered it a form of tyranny.

So the colonists decided to challenge the king. In a Williamsburg courtroom, the House of Burgesses and the ministers clashed. Defending the House, and in a sense all colonists, was a brilliant young lawyer who impressed Jefferson a great deal. He was Patrick Henry. Seven years older than Jefferson, Henry was a gifted orator and had managed to pass the bar exam after studying law for only six weeks. In a series of fiery speeches, Henry won the Parson's Case by effectively arguing that the king had no right to throw out the laws made by the Virginia legislature. Jefferson was present when an overjoyed crowd of colonists cheered Henry and carried him through the streets on their shoulders.

In the following few years, Jefferson and Henry, who became good friends, talked often of what they saw as the natural rights of citizens. Among these rights were freedom of expression and the right to self-government. Kings and other leaders, the two believed, should not be able to take away these rights at will. Furthermore, the people should make and amend their laws as they see fit. "Men are not handicapped by laws passed a hundred or a thousand years ago," said Henry. "Men live in their own times and rule themselves according to their times. Men make laws and change them when need be. But above all the laws they make, there are certain rights that no legislature can ever set aside and that be-

The fiery oratory of a brilliant young lawyer named Patrick Henry gave the colonists a legal victory against the British king. Henry's impassioned speech also impressed Jefferson and the two men became friends.

Jefferson avidly read the work of philosopher John Locke. Locke wrote that governments should be established by consent of the people rather than by the whims of monarchs.

long to every man the day he is born." When Jefferson asked what Henry thought was the most important of these rights, Henry replied, "The right to be free."[14]

Deeply impressed by the views of Henry and other patriotic colonists, Jefferson read every book he could find on the subject of government. Among these where the works of John Locke and other European thinkers who argued that governments should be established by the consent of the people rather than by the whims of monarchs. Once Jefferson had accumulated a vast array of knowledge on many subjects, he focused on ideas about freedom and fair government. The young man began to form strong opinions on these subjects, opinions he would later voice stirringly in the historic Declaration of Independence.

2 Rebellion in the Wind

The decade from the mid-1760s to the mid-1770s was one of the most turbulent and important in American history. During these years, the people in the American colonies became increasingly restless and angry with the British government. The colonists objected to the mother country meddling in local affairs and opposed many British taxes. These resentments grew into a desire for self-rule, and the colonists greeted even the slightest British provocation with open hostility. Eventually, the colonists declared their independence, broke away from Great Britain, and established a new nation with a government run by the people.

Jefferson agreed with and joined the leaders of this growing colonial revolutionary movement. Because of his considerable talents and compelling personality, he quickly became one of its leaders. All of the movement's political beliefs and activities during these years were based on what was, in an age of kings and queens, a radical principle. As Jefferson put it, "Whenever any form of government becomes destructive, it is the right of the people to alter or abolish it."[15]

Yet even as he supported the growing revolutionary movement, like many other colonists, Jefferson had doubts about its course of action. He said more than once

An angry group of colonists pulls down a statue of King George III. Many colonists engaged in daring acts of defiance to show their growing resentment toward the British government.

that he would be happy to remain a British subject, if only the king would act more fairly and put more power in the hands of the people. He sincerely hoped that the British government and colonists could reach an agreement. But Jefferson eventually acknowledged that compromise was impossible. For Jefferson and his compatriots, this left only one possible option—the colonies must become independent.

One Dispute After Another

In the following few years, many disputes arose between Great Britain and the thirteen American colonies. Patrick Henry and other colonial spokesmen became increasingly vocal about not wanting the king interfering in their local affairs. Many colonists felt that they were ready to govern themselves. Andrew Burnaby, a British traveler who visited the colonies in 1759, witnessed the growing revolutionary spirit among Virginians and other colonists. Burnaby described them as "haughty [proud], and jealous of their liberties, impatient of restraint [holding their tempers], and can scarcely bear the thought of being controlled by any superior power."[16] The colonists maintained that they could take care of themselves without British help. They especially objected to the British troops stationed in the colonies, and colonial leaders called for the British to remove these garrisons.

But the British ignored the protests and demands. The king not only ordered that the garrisons remain but also insisted that the colonists contribute to the support of the British troops. The British legislature, called Parliament, chose to make the

Colonists were outraged by the Stamp Act, which required a stamp (pictured) on all documents. Money from the sale of stamps supported British troops stationed in the colonies.

colonists pay for the troops by imposing the Stamp Act in 1765. This law forced the colonists to buy a stamp for almost every kind of document they used, from licenses and court papers to newspapers and college diplomas. The colonists believed the tax unfair because they had no representation in Parliament and so had no means of appealing the act. A majority of people in all thirteen colonies were outraged. Jefferson was in the audience in the House of Burgesses when his friend Patrick Henry stood up to denounce British colonial policy in general and the Stamp Act in particular. When a British sympathizer accused Henry of treason, Henry defiantly fired back, "If this be treason, make the most of it!" Jefferson never forgot the electrifying effect Henry's oratory had on the colonists during these years. Later, Jefferson credited Henry with setting "the ball of revolution" in motion.

Rising Tensions Lead to Bloodshed

Colonial leaders protested so loudly against the Stamp Act that Parliament repealed it in 1766. But a year later, the British imposed a new series of taxes through the Townshend Acts. Tea, paper, ink, and glass now carried heavy taxes. The colonists became angrier than ever, and in 1769, the Virginia House of Burgesses passed resolutions demanding that the British leave decisions about taxes to the colonies themselves. Jefferson helped pass these defiant resolutions. He had been admitted to the bar in 1767 and then gained election to the House of Burgesses in 1768 at the age of twenty-five. By 1769, he was already one of the most popular and respected members of the legislature. He was also one of the most vocal opponents of British attempts to dictate local colonial policies. He and his colleagues were appalled and insulted

An eighteenth-century artist depicts the growing tension between the colonists and Britain. Boston colonists grin broadly while tarring and feathering a British tax collector.

The repeal of the Stamp Act did not soothe angry colonists, whose ire increased when Britain imposed new taxes on tea, paper, ink, and glass. Colonists' anger was often visited upon tax collectors, as this photo shows.

when the king's local governor responded to the new resolutions by dissolving the House of Burgesses.

Jefferson and other colonial leaders refused to be intimidated. The Virginia lawmakers continued to meet in secret and vowed not to buy any goods taxed by Parliament. Leaders in the other colonies quickly followed their example. Tensions steadily rose until a group of angry colonists clashed with British troops in Boston in 1770. Several colonists were killed and wounded. The news of what became known as the Boston Massacre spread swiftly through the colonies and provoked widespread resentment against the British.

Jefferson, who had hoped that the king and Parliament might act more reasonably, now believed that British rule had become tyrannical and dangerous. Along with Patrick Henry and leaders in other colonies, Jefferson helped set up committees of correspondence, which were lines of communication intended to spread news of the latest British offenses among the various colonies. The committees were important because they marked the first time that all the colonies worked together against the British.

News accounts told of the fate that befell the dead and wounded and urged the colonists to stand strong against their British foe.

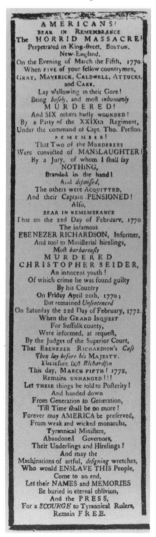

Colonists and British troops battle in Boston in March 1770. Five colonists were killed and six wounded in what came to be known as the Boston Massacre.

A Desire to Settle Down

The legislature, committees of correspondence, and other political activities occupied only part of Jefferson's time during these years. He also devoted many hours each week to his law practice. In addition, he began building a new home near Shadwell. Its location was on a beautiful hilltop that he and his close friend Dabney Carr had discovered as boys. At that time, Carr thought the location so lovely that he expressed the desire to be buried there someday. Jefferson vowed that he would build a magnificent house on the spot. Now in his twenties, Jefferson was ready to fulfill that vow and begin building what he called Monticello, which means "little mountain" in Italian. Historian Merrill D. Peterson describes the beginning stages of what became a lifelong project:

> He began sawing lumber and planting fruit trees in 1767; the next year he let a contract [hired workers] to level the summit [of the hill]; and in 1769 the foundations were dug, the brick kilns fired, and hardware ordered from England. . . . He became his own architect. The versatility he demonstrated in this endeavor marked a permanent trait, exploding in all directions. . . . Others might be content with what was; he could think only in terms of what should be. . . . To build a house with any pretensions to elegance in this remote country was difficult. But to rear it on a densely wooded summit seemed an act of folly. There was no precedent for it in America or in England. . . . The simplest explanation is that he liked

In November 1770 Jefferson moved into Monticello, his dream house. The continual renovation of Monticello remained one of Jefferson's lifelong passions.

> the view. . . . The place appealed to his . . . sense of the beautiful and sublime. . . . The house itself was completed in about a dozen years . . . [and] Jefferson rebuilt Monticello along its present lines in the 1790s. In a sense, he was always building Monticello. It was a lifelong passion, not simply as an object of taste and beauty but as an object of workmanship.[17]

Though the house was far from finished, Jefferson moved into it in November 1770, primarily because a devastating fire had destroyed the house at Shadwell a few months before. "I have here but one room," he wrote in a letter, "which, like the cobbler's, serves me for parlor, for kitchen and hall . . . for bed chamber and study too."[18] He now had an incentive to speed up the building process.

Jefferson soon had another reason for finishing Monticello. Late in 1770, he began courting Martha Wayles Skelton, a twenty-three-year-old widow who lived

A Book Lover

In 1770, a fire destroyed the Jefferson house at Shadwell. Jefferson lost most of his books, papers, and letters. That these items were more important to him than most things, including money, is apparent in the following letter he wrote to his friend John Page:

"My late loss may perhaps have reached you by this time, I mean the loss of my mother's house by fire, and in it of every paper I had in the world, and almost every book. On a reasonable estimate I calculate the cost of the books to have been 200 sterling. Would to god it had been the money; then had it never cost me a sigh! To make the loss more sensible it fell principally on my books of common law, of which I have but one left, at that time lent out. Of papers too of every kind I am utterly destitute. All of these, whether public or private, of business or amusement, have perished in the flames. I had made some progress in preparing for the succeeding general court, and having, as was my custom, thrown my thoughts into the form of notes, I troubled my head no more with them. These are gone, and 'like the baseless fabric of a vision, Leave not a trace behind' [his paraphrase of a line from Shakespeare's *The Tempest*]."

Some of Jefferson's law books. Jefferson was deeply saddened when a fire at Shadwell resulted in the loss of many of his books.

Martha Skelton married Jefferson in 1772. She was charming, well-educated, and an avid reader.

near Williamsburg. They were attracted to each other at first because they shared a love of music. For years, Jefferson had told his friends he enjoyed being a bachelor and that he would probably never marry. But meeting a woman as cultured and versatile as Martha changed his mind. Although Jefferson never described her in writing, his great-granddaughter, Sarah N. Randolph, reported:

> She is described as having been very beautiful. A little above middle height, with . . . an exquisitely formed figure, she was a model of graceful and queenlike carriage. Nature, so lavish with her charms for her, to great personal attractions, added a mind of no ordinary calibre [quality]. She was well-educated for her day, and a constant reader.[19]

On New Year's Day in 1772, Jefferson and Martha Skelton were married at The Forest, her home near Williamsburg. They immediately departed for Monticello to

Interior view of Monticello. Martha and Thomas spent their honeymoon there although only one room had been completed by that time.

An Advocate for Justice

Jefferson was appalled by the way the colonists often treated the Indians. In April 1774, a group of whites murdered the entire family of a Shawnee chief named Logan, who was known to be a friend of the whites. Logan retaliated and was later captured. Logan spoke in his own defense and Jefferson, who witnessed the speech, immediately jotted it down. It is taken from Jefferson's The Virginia Almanac, *published in 1775.*

"I appeal to any white man to say, if ever he entered Logan's cabin hungry, and he gave him not meat; if ever he came cold and naked, and he clothed him not. During the course of the last long and bloody war Logan remained idle in his cabin, an advocate for peace. Such was my love for the whites, that my countrymen pointed as they passed, and said, 'Logan is the friend of white men.' I had even thought to have lived with you, but for the injuries of one man. Colonel Cresap, the last spring, in cold blood, and unprovoked, murdered all the relations of Logan, not even sparing my women and children. There runs not a drop of my blood in the veins of any living creature. This called on me for revenge. I have sought it: I have killed many: I have fully glutted my vengeance: for my country I rejoice at the beams of peace. But do not harbour a thought that mine is the joy of fear. Logan never felt fear. He will not turn on his heel [run away] to save his life. Who is there to mourn for Logan?—Not one."

spend their honeymoon. Years later, their daughter Martha recalled hearing from Jefferson how the couple

> left The Forest after a fall of snow, light then, but increasing in depth as they advanced up the country. They were finally obliged to quit the carriage and proceed on horseback. Having stopped for a short time . . . [they made] their way through a mountain track [path] rather than a road, in which the snow lay from eighteen inches to two feet deep, having eight miles to go before reaching Monticello. They arrived late at night, the fires all out and the servants retired to their own houses for the night.[20]

Jefferson's one completed room, he said, became his "Honeymoon Lodge."

Jefferson greatly enjoyed the quiet days he spent with his new wife at Monticello, and he found working on the house both challenging and relaxing. He often said that his greatest goal in life was to settle down on that lovely hilltop and pursue the peaceful intellectual pastimes that interested him. But during the early 1770s, he found fewer chances to slip away from

Williamsburg to the countryside. His intelligence, talents, and devotion to the revolutionary cause made him indispensable to his fellow patriots.

War Is the Only Choice

One of Jefferson's most important contributions to the Revolution was the result of a chain of events that began in Boston in 1773. One night, a group of Bostonians dressed up like Indians and dumped a large load of tea into the harbor. They did this to protest the heavy tax on tea. Parliament retaliated in 1774 by passing a set of measures that restricted many colonial rights. For instance, the British closed Boston Harbor to all commerce, limited the local governing powers of colonial town meetings, and forced many private home owners to house and feed British troops. The colonists referred to these measures as the Intolerable Acts. In June 1774, incensed over these acts, the colonies sent representatives to a special congress, or meeting, in Philadelphia. This Continental Congress would be a legislative body that would take any action necessary against further British oppression.

In preparation for the Continental Congress, Jefferson's colleagues asked him to write down on paper a summary of the colonists' grievances against the king. The purpose of the document was to inform both the colonists and the British of the colonial leaders' official position. In the document, called *A Summary View of the Rights of British America,* Jefferson argued that nature had given all peoples the right to establish their own government and laws. He called upon the king to act in a reasonable manner and grant the colonies a greater measure of self-rule.

Bostonians (dressed as Indians) protest Britain's tax on tea by dumping a large load of tea into Boston Harbor. Britain retaliated by closing the harbor to all commerce.

Toward Reason and Compromise

For many years before the American Revolution, Jefferson hoped that there would be no need for a violent split between the colonies and Great Britain. Jefferson stated this desire for a peaceful solution in 1774 in A Summary View of the Rights of British America. In this document, Jefferson aimed his plea for reason and compromise directly at the king:

"Kings are the servants, not the proprietors [owners] of the people. Open your breast, sire, to liberal and expanded thought. Let not the name of George the third be a blot on the page of history. . . . It behooves [is proper for] you . . . to think and to act for yourself and your people. The great principles of right and wrong are legible [clear] to every reader; to pursue them requires not the aid of many counsellors. The whole art of government consists in the art of being honest. Only aim to do your duty, and mankind will give you credit where you fail. No longer persevere [continue] in sacrificing the rights of one part of the empire to the inordinate [unreasonable] desires of another; but deal out to all equal and impartial right. . . . This is the important post in which fortune has placed you, holding the balance of a great, if a well poised empire. . . . We are willing, on our part, to sacrifice every thing which reason can ask to the restoration of that tranquillity for which all must wish. . . . This, sire, is our last, our determined resolution."

The first Continental Congress met in September 1774, and delegates voted to send their message of discontent to Great Britain by boycotting, or refusing to buy, British goods. But many colonists did not believe that economic measures would be effective. Some, like the Massachusetts minutemen, secretly began to stockpile weapons and ammunition for the fighting they were certain was to come. Their predictions proved correct when Massachusetts farmers and British troops clashed in battle in April 1775 in the Massachusetts towns of Concord and Lexington.

These violent episodes convinced most colonial patriots, including Jefferson, that the only way to solve their differences with Britain was to fight. The Continental Congress met again in the summer of 1775 and began preparing for war. That same summer, King George declared that the colonies were "engaged in open and avowed rebellion," and he made it clear he would not tolerate such impudence. The British also began war preparations. Tensions and fears mounted throughout the colonies in anticipation of the coming bloodshed. Vincent Sheean explained:

Massachusetts farmers and British troops clash in battle in April 1775 in Lexington, Massachusetts.

With things in this state, it was natural that Jefferson, already the author of . . . statements made for the American colonies, should come to the fore in Congress and should take a leading part in the decisions made. He was for independence [from Britain]. When, after the terrible confusion of a debate that seemed to have no end, the Congress decided for independence, Jefferson was asked to write the resolution [explaining why the colonies were taking up arms]. This was in June 1776. . . . Jefferson was one of a committee of five, with John Adams and others, but he alone was entrusted with the actual writing of the Declaration of Independence. He toiled over the first draft for two full days, and submitted it to Adams and [Benjamin] Franklin before he found the right form to submit to Congress. It went to Congress on June 28, was debated on July 2, 3 and 4, and was finally adopted . . . on July 4, 1776.[21]

A new nation—the United States—was born. And Thomas Jefferson, it seemed, was its official spokesman. Swept up in a whirlwind of meetings, patriotic speeches, and war preparations, Jefferson had not an inkling of the many capacities in which he would later serve that nation. He certainly did not dream that he would one day become one of its greatest leaders.

3 Architect of Freedom

In the summer of 1776, Thomas Jefferson was one of a handful of men involved in the task of establishing a new nation. It was a daring and risky venture. Great Britain was one of the mightiest nations on earth and might easily crush the rebellion. To many people in the countries of "civilized" Europe, the colonists seemed audacious and impudent in rejecting their mother country. The concepts of freedom and equality, which many colonists used to justify their rebellion, seemed odd and dangerous. Because most countries in the world were and had always been monarchies, the government based on democratic ideals that Jefferson and his colleagues envisioned was quite radical.

Although most colonists were against British colonial policies, many were not sure that breaking away from the mother country was the best way to remedy the situation. To justify the break to the colonists who were still in doubt, as well as to the world, the revolutionaries decided to draft a special document. This document would formally announce the split with Great Britain and summarize the reasons for the action.

Because of the clear and dramatic way he had expressed important ideas in the 1774 *Summary View,* Jefferson was quickly chosen for the task of writing the Declaration of Independence. In the few days he labored on the project, he wrestled with many weighty social, political, and moral

The colonists turned to Jefferson in 1776 to draft their most important document yet: the Declaration of Independence.

issues. These were issues he had thought and talked about for many years. His ideas about freedom and a government established by and for the people had evolved and developed over time. Now, pressed by the momentous events at hand, he brought his ideas and beliefs into strong, sharp focus on paper. Speaking for himself and for his fellow patriots, Jefferson helped lay the foundation for the democracy of the United States that has endured to the present.

Powerful Ideas Expressed Simply

In mid-June 1776, Jefferson sat down at his desk in one of two small rented rooms on Market Street in Philadelphia and began writing the Declaration. The desk was his own, a portable one built especially for him by a Philadelphia cabinetmaker named Benjamin Randolph. The document was a combination of ideas from many diverse sources. It was built partly on Jefferson's understanding of British law and on the concepts of philosophers like John Locke. Jefferson also incorporated arguments about equality and freedom that he had heard over the years in courtrooms, churches, and taverns. In one moving and memorable phrase after another, he committed his ideas to paper.

"We hold these truths to be self-evident," he began, "that all men are created equal; that they are endowed by their Creator with certain inalienable rights; that among these are life, liberty, and the pursuit of happiness." He went on to declare that when a government threatens these rights, "it is the right of the people to alter or to abolish it, and to institute new government." Jefferson accused the British king of abusing colonial rights. "The history of the present king of Great Britain is a history of repeated injuries

Jefferson's original draft of the Declaration of Independence. Jefferson carefully considered the wording of this most important document, making changes as he wrote to be sure it expressed clearly and precisely the views and intentions of the new nation.

A Busy Schedule

Jefferson's curiosity, appetite for learning, and sheer energy were so large that even in the crucial days leading up to the July 4, 1776, Declaration of Independence, he kept himself busy with research and other tasks. In his biography of Jefferson, historian Nathan Schachner describes a portion of the great statesman's incredibly varied schedule during those momentous days:

"During the great debate on independence and the Declaration which was to proclaim it to the world, Jefferson did not relinquish [give up] his other pursuits. On July 1st, for example, he began a detailed and meticulous series of weather observations which were continued, with but few interruptions, through most of his life. Each morning and evening he noted the exact temperature and, dissatisfied with the accuracy of his instrument, he took time on July 4th—the great day itself—to buy a new and expensive thermometer for £3, 15s. To this he added on the 8th a barometer, costing £4, 10s. As time went on, more information was jotted down in his notebooks— wind direction and velocity; the first appearance and final departure of leaves, flowers, fruits, insects and birds; observations on solar eclipses and the aurora borealis. No press of private or public business was permitted to interfere; and eventually he entered into correspondence with like-minded amateur meteorologists in other sections of the country for an interchange of information and observational data. In effect he was instituting, without quite realizing it, the first general weather bureau in the world. Nor did he forget his family at home during this trying period. On that same notable 4th of July he visited the Philadelphia purveyors of fine articles for ladies and chose seven pairs of gloves to send to Monticello and, at a later date, six pairs of shoes."

and usurpations [illegal seizures], all having in direct object the establishment of an absolute tyranny over these states." After listing these injuries, Jefferson concluded with the all-important statement of independence:

We, therefore, the representatives of the United States of America . . . do in the name, and by the authority of the good people of these colonies, solemnly publish and declare, that these untied colonies are, and of right ought to be free and independent states. . . . And for the support of this declaration, we mutually pledge to each other our lives, our fortunes, and our sacred honor.[22]

The Declaration of Independence

The Declaration of Independence, written by Jefferson in June 1776, remains one of the greatest documents expressing the desire for human freedom and equality ever written:

"We hold these truths to be self-evident: that all men are created equal; that they are endowed by their Creator with certain inalienable rights; that among these are life, liberty, and the pursuit of happiness; that to secure these rights, governments are instituted among men, deriving their just powers from the consent of the governed; that whenever any form of government becomes destructive of these ends, it is the right of the people to alter or to abolish it, and to institute new government, laying its foundation on such principles, and organizing its powers in such form, as to them shall seem most likely to effect their safety and happiness. . . .

The history of the present king of Great Britain is a history of repeated injuries and usurpations, all having in direct object the establishment of an absolute tyranny over these states. To prove this, let facts be submitted to a candid world. He has refused to assent to laws the most wholesome and necessary for the public good. . . . He has dissolved representative houses [legislatures] repeatedly for opposing with manly firmness his invasions on the rights of the people. . . . He has kept among us in times of peace standing armies without the consent of our legislatures. . . . He has plundered our seas, ravaged our coasts, burnt our towns, and destroyed the lives of our people. . . .

We, therefore, the representatives of the United States of America in General Congress assembled, appealing to the supreme judge of the world [God] for the rectitude [rightness] of our intentions, do in the name, and by the authority of the good people of these colonies, solemnly publish and declare, that these united colonies are, and of right ought to be free and independent states; that they are absolved from all allegiance to the British crown, and that all political connection between them and the state of Great Britain is, and ought to be, totally dissolved; and that as free and independent states. . . . And for the support of this declaration, we mutually pledge to each other our lives, our fortunes, and our sacred honor."

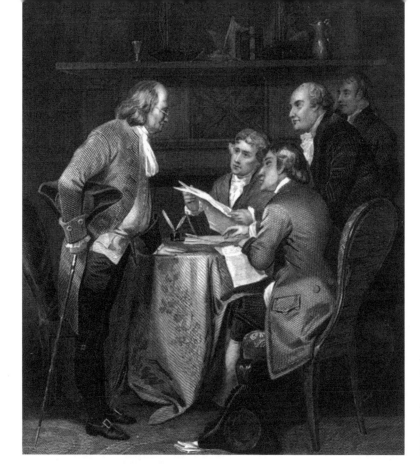

A committee of delegates to the Continental Congress discusses Jefferson's draft. Among the committee members are Benjamin Franklin (left) and Jefferson (seated, holding the draft).

Jefferson later recalled that after finishing the first draft of the Declaration: "I communicated it separately to Dr. [Benjamin] Franklin and Mr. [John] Adams, requesting their corrections, because they were the two . . . of whose judgments and amendments I wished most to have the benefit. . . . Their alterations were two or three only, and merely verbal. I then wrote a fair [readable] copy, [and] reported it . . . unaltered, to Congress."[23]

On July 2, 1776, the Continental Congress began debating what and how much of the wording of the Declaration might need to be changed. Most delegates were moved by the way Jefferson had stated important and powerful ideas so clearly and simply. Dramatic and eloquent as the document was, however, the delegates did feel that some changes were in order. For two days, Jefferson watched as his colleagues made revisions to his original draft.

Seeing that Jefferson was disturbed by what was happening, Benjamin Franklin, the well-known Philadelphia diplomat, newspaperman, and inventor, who was then seventy, took the younger man aside. Jefferson should learn a lesson from this, the wise and kindly Franklin explained. "I have made it a rule," said Franklin, "whenever in my power, to avoid becoming the draughtsman [writer] of papers to be reviewed by a public body. I took my lesson from an incident I will relate to you."[24] Franklin then told the story of a hatmaker who proposed a detailed sign to hang above his shop and asked his friends for advice. They proceeded to eliminate all of what he considered his best wording and left only his name and the picture of a hat. Jefferson remembered with humor this conversation with Franklin in a letter more than forty years later, long after the older man's death. Jefferson also looked back thankfully on the many other times Franklin offered him helpful advice during their two decades of friendship.

The Great Document Approved and Signed

For the most part, the changes the delegates made in the Declaration were minor. They toned down some of Jefferson's harsh denunciations of the king, fearing these might incite the British to war sooner rather than later. They also inserted several references to God, which Jefferson considered unnecessary. These changes bothered Jefferson only slightly. He was particularly upset, however, when the delegates deleted an entire paragraph in which he described slavery as an evil institution that should be eliminated. In his original draft, Jefferson had written:

> He [the king] has waged cruel war against human nature itself, violating its most sacred rights of life and liberty in the persons of distant people, who never offended him, captivating [capturing] and carrying them into slavery in another hemisphere, or to incur miserable death in their transportation thither. . . . Determined to keep open a market where Men should be bought and sold, he has prostituted his negative for suppressing every legislative attempt to prohibit or restrain this execrable [horrible] commerce.[25]

Jefferson's use of a capital letter in the word *Men* to describe the slaves was meant to emphasize that the slaves were human beings just like their masters. In a way, this point summed up his entire argument

Debate over the exact wording of the Declaration of Independence concluded on July 4, 1776. Delegates to the Continental Congress gathered a month later for the momentous signing of the document.

On Slavery

By today's standards, Jefferson's actions regarding his own slaves appear to contradict his publicly stated moral views. For Jefferson, however, there was no contradiction. He felt that his slaves would not be able to support themselves on their own and that as free blacks, they would encounter cruel prejudice. Therefore, he believed that keeping and supporting his slaves was more humane than freeing them. In his Notes on the State of Virginia, *written in 1781, Jefferson made his moral objections to slavery clear:*

"There must doubtless be an unhappy influence on the manners of our people produced by the existence of slavery among us. The whole commerce between master and slave is a perpetual exercise of the most boisterous passions [emotions], the most unremitting despotism [tyranny] on the one part, and degrading submissions on the other. Our children see this, and learn to imitate it; for man is an imitative animal. This quality is the germ of all education in him. From his cradle to his grave he is learning to do what he sees others do. . . . The parent storms [yells at the slaves], the child looks on . . . puts on the same airs in the circle of smaller [younger] slaves, gives a loose to his worst of passions, and thus nursed, educated, and daily exercised in tyranny, cannot but be stamped by it. . . . And with what execration [hatred] should the statesman be loaded, who permitting one half the citizens thus to trample on the rights of the other, transforms those [the owners] into despots [tyrants], and these [the slaves] into enemies, destroys the morals of the one part, and the amor patriae [love for one's country] of the other. For if a slave can have a country in this world, it must be any other in preference to that in which he is born to live and labour for another. . . . I think change already perceptible. . . . The spirit of the master is abating [receding], that of the slave rising from the dust, his condition mollifying [easing], the way I hope preparing . . . for a total emancipation, and that this is disposed [destined] in the order of events, to be with the consent [rather than the destruction] of the masters."

about slavery: the buying and selling of human beings was repulsive, and the new nation should not tolerate it. But many of Jefferson's colleagues did not agree. Southern delegates, especially those from South Carolina and Georgia whose economies were dependent on the labor of slaves, voted to ban the reference to slavery. Many Northerners, believing the economies of the North and South were dependent on each other, voted with them. History later proved that Jefferson's heart and mind had

The Declaration of Independence, revered worldwide for its simplicity, clarity, and powerful expression of the desire for human freedom and equality.

An 1880 illustration depicts triumphant members of Congress leaving Independence Hall after the first public reading of the Declaration of Independence.

been in the right place. The failure of the founders to eliminate slavery in the beginning had serious consequences for the country later when the Union became divided by a bloody civil war over the same issue.

Late in the afternoon on July 4, 1776, the debate concluded and the delegates approved the Declaration. A printer named John Dunlop produced copies the next day, and the delegates distributed them to their respective assemblies. On August 2, the Congress met again to sign the Declaration. Along with Jefferson, some of the fifty-five other distinguished citizens who placed their names at the bottom of the document were John Adams, Samuel Adams, Benjamin Franklin, John Penn, George Wythe, and John Hancock.

Jefferson, like the others, knew that the British now viewed him as a traitor and that he might one day forfeit his life for these actions. But he had committed himself to what he saw as a just and noble cause, and he intended to stick to that commitment no matter what. It was up to the British to make the next move. For the time being, Jefferson felt, he had done his duty to his country. On September 1, 1776, he climbed on his horse and rode to Monticello, anxious to resume his duties at home.

The Role of Intellectual Leader

But soon, Jefferson found his restful solitude in the country interrupted again. During the next few years, the infant United States waged a desperate, bloody war with Great Britain, and Jefferson's colleagues once more called him into service. His contributions were not on the battlefield, however. From 1776 to 1779, he served as a legislator in the Virginia assembly. There, he did much more than propose laws and make policy for his state. Jefferson soon assumed the unofficial role of intellectual leader and thinker for the young nation. In discussions with his colleagues, in his writings, and in the assembly, he dealt with the most important social, political, and moral issues of the day. Perhaps the most important question he faced was what would happen when the fighting was over. What exactly was a democracy "of and by the people"? And how would the new country actually put such a seemingly radical ideal into practice?

These are the questions Jefferson tried to answer in the late 1770s and early 1780s. He tried diligently to make the government of his state a model for the national government the revolutionaries planned to create after the fighting was over. The architect of Monticello now strived to be an architect of a new kind of society, one based on freedom and equality of opportunity. He did not always succeed in bringing about the radical changes he desired. His attempts to eradicate slavery, for instance, were as unsuccessful in the Virginia assembly as they had been at the Continental Congress. But so important was his influence on his fellow patriots that many of the ideas he introduced at this time gained acceptance and helped shape the course of the nation in the next few decades.

For example, not all of Jefferson's colleagues shared his democratic ideas about social status, the idea of a natural aristocracy based solely on virtue and talent. Many of the nation's founders were wealthy members of the landed aristocracy, and they enjoyed the special rights and privileges this status brought. For generations, large tracts of land had been controlled by single, wealthy families simply by right of birth. This helped to keep much of the country's wealth and power in the hands of a few aristocrats. In the Virginia

assembly, Jefferson argued vigorously for and won legislation making some of this land available for purchase to people of lesser means.

An important step in this process was eliminating the traditional right of primogeniture. This was the right of the first-born male in a family to inherit his father's entire estate, and this tended to keep large estates from breaking up and becoming distributed among several owners. "I proposed to abolish the law of primogeniture," Jefferson later wrote, "and to make real estate descendible in parcenary [to be inherited in separate portions] to the next of kin . . . by the statute of distribution." [26]

Like many other laws Jefferson helped pass during these years, those making land available to more people had an important effect on the later development of the

Jefferson argued vigorously against laws that kept land in the hands of a few powerful aristocrats.

The Virginia Constitution

The Declaration of Independence became Jefferson's most famous piece of writing, and many people do not realize that he composed an equally eloquent and important document in the same month he wrote the Declaration. This was the Virginia Constitution, *designed to replace the old colonial version. In the preamble, he listed the abuses inflicted on the colonists by King George:*

"Whereas George . . . king of Great Britain and Ireland . . . heretofore [before this] entrusted with the exercise of the kingly office in this government hath endeavored to pervert the same into a detestable and insupportable tyranny;

by putting his negative on laws the most wholesome & necessary for ye public good;

by denying to his governors permission to pass laws of immediate and pressing importance . . . ;

by dissolving legislative assemblies repeatedly and continually for opposing with manly firmness his invasions on the rights of the people . . . ;

by keeping among us in times of peace, standing armies and ships of war . . . ;

for quartering large bodies of troops among us;

for cutting off our trade with all parts of the world;

for imposing taxes on us without our consent;

for depriving us of the benefits of trial by jury . . . ;

by plundering our seas, ravaging our coasts, burning our towns, and destroying the lives of our people . . . ;

by transporting at this time a large army of foreign mercenaries to complete the works of death, desolation & tyranny already begun . . . ;

by answering our repeated petitions for redress [remedy] with a repetition of injuries;

and finally by abandoning the helm of government and declaring us out of his allegiance and protection . . .

said George has forfeited the kingly office and rendered it necessary . . . that he should be immediately deposed [removed] from the same."

---

nation. These laws opened the way for small farmers to move into the western frontier. Jefferson saw the small farmer as the ultimate natural aristocrat because such a farmer earned the right to own land through talent, ability, and hard work. Other prominent Virginians like James Madison and politician John Taylor agreed with their friend Jefferson. Historian Irwin Unger explained:

These men cherished the idea of an agricultural society of small freeholders led by landed gentlemen [like Jefferson and Madison]. According to Jefferson, the farmers of the nation, were the "chosen people of God, if ever he had a chosen people." By contrast, the artisans, journeymen, and laborers who made up the "mobs" of the cities were "the panders [exploiters] of vice and the instruments by which the liberties of a country are generally overturned." . . . The agrarian [farming] appeal is easy to explain. Simplicity, self-sufficiency, and the natural life strike a deep chord in most people. And for Americans, agrarianism was particularly attractive. . . . Throughout history, country dwellers have disdained [rejected] commerce and industry and distrusted cities and towns

Like Jefferson, James Madison had high regard for farmers who earned the right to own land through talent, ability, and hard work.

and their inhabitants. What passed for political wisdom reinforced the rural prejudice. Had not [John] Locke and other thinkers who strongly influenced the revolutionary generation established that those who owned land were the most honest and independent citizens?[27]

Education and Religion

Another issue that Jefferson debated in the Virginia assembly was education. He and some of his colleagues wanted to ensure that in a system ruled by the people, everyone was equipped to take part in government. In order to cast meaningful votes or to run for office, people had to be able to read about, understand, and debate important issues. Jefferson believed that education was the key. In fact, he believed that without an effective system of public education, the country could not remain a free society. "If a nation expects to be ignorant and free in a state of civilization," he stated, "it expects what never was and never will be."[28] He proposed to the Virginia assembly that the state sponsor a widespread educational system and that it also build free libraries for the use of the people. In addition, he advocated giving gifted children special training to increase the pool of leaders, scientists, inventors, and thinkers. Unfortunately, Virginia found Jefferson's education plan too ambitious and expensive.

Jefferson also fought hard for the separation of church and state. Christian churches were very powerful in Virginia, as they were in other sections of the country. Often, the taxes people paid supported these churches and paid the ministers' salaries. This practice had been at the root of the dispute in the 1763 Parson's Case. Jefferson believed in God, but he also believed it wrong for organized religions to impose themselves on the people. And government, if it is to represent all the people, should not take an official religious view by supporting a particular faith, financially or otherwise. In his opinion, this forced society, and therefore the individuals who make up society, to support a certain religion. This support, he said, should be a private, not a public, matter. No one should be judged on the basis of which church he or she supports, nor should someone be judged for choosing to support no church at all. In other words, there should be both freedom *of* religion and freedom *from* religion. In *Notes on the State of Virginia,* written in 1785, Jefferson said:

It does me no injury for my neighbor to say there are twenty gods, or no god. It neither picks my pocket nor breaks my leg. . . . Millions of innocent men, women, and children, since the introduction of Christianity, have been burnt, tortured, fined, imprisoned; yet we have not advanced one inch toward uniformity [of belief]. What has been the effect of coercion [forcing people to accept religion]? To make one half the world fools, and other half hypocrites. To support roguery [crime] and error all over the earth. Let us reflect that it is inhabited by a thousand million people. That these profess probably a thousand different religions. That ours is but one of a thousand. That if there be but one right, and ours that one, we should wish to

see the 999 wandering sects gathered into the fold of truth. But . . . we cannot effect this by force. Reason and persuasion are the only practicable instruments. . . . The way to silence religious disputes is to take no notice of them. Let us . . . give this experiment fair play, and get rid, while we may, of those tyrannical laws [binding church and state].[29]

Jefferson proposed his Bill for Establishing Religious Freedom in the Virginia assembly in 1779. "Be it therefore enacted by the General Assembly," he worded the ending of the document, "that no man shall be compelled to frequent or support any religious worship, place or ministry whatsoever, nor shall be enforced, restrained, molested, or burthened [burdened], nor shall otherwise suffer on account of his religious opinions or belief."[30] After intermittent debate for several years, the bill passed in 1786. Jefferson considered it one of his greatest achievements, and it became a model for similar bills in other states.

As the war with Great Britain continued, Jefferson remained as active as ever. When he was not pressing for reforms in the assembly in Williamsburg or arguing philosophical points with Madison, Adams, and other colleagues, he was busy at Monticello. He spent time with Martha and their daughter, also named Martha, who had been born in 1772. He also found time to plant orange trees, study lightning bugs, observe celestial eclipses, and work on his house. He looked forward to the war's end with the fervent hope that at last he would be able to retire to these leisure activities for good. Once more, he would be disappointed.

4 The Reluctant Diplomat

During and immediately after the Revolution, Thomas Jefferson continued to serve his country in a series of important public posts. Between 1779 and 1800, he served as governor of Virginia, as a congressman, as minister to France, as secretary of state, and as vice-president. As in the past, the roles of politician and diplomat did not appeal to Jefferson nearly as much as those of farmer, inventor, naturalist, and architect. He would have preferred to spend most of his time tinkering with his various projects at Monticello. Many times during these years, he expressed the desire to retire from politics. For example, after his term as Virginia's governor ended, he vowed he would never again hold public office, having "retired to my farm, my family and books from which I think nothing will ever more separate me."[31]

But Jefferson repeatedly broke this vow. The insistence of his colleagues that he serve and his own interest in the well-being of the new nation drew him back to the public arena time and again. All the while, he remained a key figure in the creation of the country's government, laws, ideals, and goals.

The War Governor

Jefferson's distinguished service in the Virginia assembly during the early years of the war convinced most Virginia legislators that he would make a good governor. They appointed him to that post in June 1779 when he was thirty-six. Feeling that his fellow citizens needed him, Jefferson accepted the post and pledged to do his best. But he knew full well that he had taken control of the state government at the worst possible time. The British were in the process of invading Virginia. The state's treasury was almost empty, and there was little hope of raising money through taxes. After all, the people's opposition to taxation had been one of the principal causes of the Revolution.

To make matters worse, the state militia, consisting mainly of small farmers, was poorly trained, equipped, and supplied. Jefferson spent much of his time as governor trying to recruit new troops, scrounging for supplies, and consulting with his military commanders about the best ways to defend the state. Congress could do little or nothing to help Virginia or any other the region. The militia could do little to stop them. After losing skirmish after skirmish, the Virginia militia's morale sank, and many militiamen deserted. In January 1781, the British entered and burned Richmond, which had recently become the new state capital. This forced Jefferson and other leaders to flee into the countryside.

A few months later, with Virginia's defenses still in disarray, the commander of the British forces, Lord Charles Cornwallis, saw the chance to totally defeat and humiliate the Virginians. He ordered Col. Bonastre Tarleton to chase down and capture Jefferson and his fellow assemblymen.

On orders from the commander of British forces, Col. Bonastre Tarleton raced to Monticello in hopes of capturing Jefferson and other Virginia leaders.

George Washington commanded America's first army. The army had priority over the Virginia militia when it came to troops, supplies, and equipment.

state at the time. The national army under George Washington was the country's top priority for receiving troops, supplies, and equipment. In fact, Jefferson often had to divert some of his own vitally needed men and supplies to Washington's army.

For two years, Jefferson, his commanders, and the Virginia militia faced nearly overwhelming odds. In 1779, the British landed eighteen hundred seasoned troops at Hampton Roads, Virginia. These redcoats looted and burned the crops and towns of

Jefferson's term as governor had expired only days before, but because no new governor had been appointed, he was still the state's most important public figure. With about 250 men, Tarleton raced toward Monticello, where he knew Jefferson was sheltering many of the assemblymen. At the last minute, one of Jefferson's friends rode at top speed through backwoods trails to Monticello and sounded a warning. Most of the assemblymen then fled toward nearby Charlottesville. Historian Nathan Schachner recalled what happened next:

> Dispatching Captain McLeod to Monticello to capture Jefferson, Tarleton pursued the fleeing assemblymen and destroyed all stores in Charlottesville. . . . Meanwhile Jefferson was unaccountably dilatory [slow]. He was still gathering up his papers, and his family were still on the grounds, when one Christopher Hudson [another of Jefferson's friends] . . . galloped up the mountain to warn Jefferson [about McLeod's approach]. This time Jefferson acted with speed. He sent his family away at once. . . . Making some last-minute arrangements, which were almost too late, he mounted a horse. By now, McLeod's dragoons [troops] were painfully visible coming up the mountain, and Jefferson spurred [galloped at full speed] into the woods. . . . Five or ten minutes later the dragoons stood on the level plateau of Monticello to find their prey escaped. . . . McLeod proved a gentleman. He remained on the grounds for eighteen hours before he descended to rejoin the main force; but during that time nothing was taken and nothing was harmed.[32]

Intellectual Triumph and Personal Tragedy

Soon after Jefferson's last-minute escape, he and his family managed to reach safety. At first, it appeared that the British would subdue the whole state and Jefferson would remain a fugitive on the run. But within a few months, the tide of war changed significantly. The French, who had begun helping the Americans against Great Britain in

Gen. Marquis de Lafayette of France proved to be an important friend of the colonists at the battle of Yorktown.

The British surrender their arms to Washington in 1781 after their defeat at Yorktown.

The battle of Yorktown was a bitter defeat for Britain's esteemed General Cornwallis.

1778, landed a fleet near the Virginia coast. This trapped the British between the sea and the advancing American troops led by Washington. Assisted by the French general, the Marquis de Lafayette, Washington defeated General Cornwallis at Yorktown, Virginia, on October 19, 1781. A few months after this major American victory, the British decided not to pursue the war any further and opened peace negotiations. The thirteen colonies had won their war of independence.

Like his fellow revolutionaries, Jefferson was excited by and tremendously proud of the American victory. His long-awaited return to private life after the war also pleased him greatly. Once settled at Monticello, he began the complex task of recording his opinions on a wide range of topics. He wrote a remarkable book entitled *Notes on the State of Virginia,* which reflected the

THE COLONIAL GAZETTE.

Num. 39.]　　　　　　　　SUPPLEMENT.　　　　　　Price 2 Pence

Oct.　　　　　　　　　　　　　　　　　　1781

LETTER FROM GEN. WASHINGTON TO THE GOVERNOR OF MARYLAND, ANNOUNCING THE SURRENDER OF CORNWALLIS.

CAMP NEAR YORK, OCT., 1781.

DEAR SIR : Inclosed I have the honor of transmitting to your Excellency the terms upon which Lord Cornwallis has surrendered the Garrisons of York and Gloucester.

We have not been able yet to get an account of prisoners, ordnance or stores in the different departments : but from the best general report there will be (officers included) upwards of seven thousand men, besides seamen, more than 70 pieces of brass ordnance and a hundred of iron, their stores and other valuable articles.

My present engagements will not allow me to add more than my congratulations on this happy event, and to express the high sense I have of the powerful aid which I have derived from the State of Maryland in complying with my every request to the execution of it. The prisoners will be divided between Winchester, in Virginia, and Fort Frederick, in Maryland. With every sentiment of the most perfect esteem and regard, I have the honor to be

Your Excellency's most obedient and humble servant,　　　　　G. WASHINGTON.

The French at Yorktown.

Few things, indeed, suggested by the history of the war are more instructive than a parallel between the fate of Burgoyne and the fate of Cornwallis. The defeat of Washington on Long Island and the loss of New York had been attributed to the fact that his troops were raw militia. Yet it was mainly with just such men, and not with Continentals (as the regular soldiers of the united colonies were called), that the American commanders in northern New York overcame, in two successive battles, the well-disciplined and admirably appointed army of Burgoyne. This was the one brilliant military triumph achieved by either party in the whole course of the struggle; yet, strange to say, its most substantial fruit was its favorable effect on the negotiations which for two years Franklin had been pushing at the court of Versailles. It was not, however, until the beginning of the ensuing year that the French Ministry would even promise assistance to the colonies; and although their advances of money may from that time forward be said to have kept the continental army on its feet, they did not render effective military aid until the arrival of Count De Grasse in the Chesapeake, about the beginning of September, 1781.

The surrender of Cornwallis was the direct result of the advantage gained by De Grasse over Admiral Graves in the naval battle which took place off the mouth of Chesapeake Bay on September 5, 1781. For the first time during the war, the English failed to have a preponderance of naval strength in American waters, and for almost the first time an English Admiral, commanding a force not greatly inferior to his opponents, sailed pusillanimously away after an indecisive action, in which the French loss in killed and wounded was actually the greater. After this unexpected and inexcusable behaviour on the part of an English naval officer, the surrender of Cornwallis was clearly an obvious necessity. On one side there was the French fleet, comprising twenty four ships of the line carrying 1,700 guns, and 19,000 seamen. On the land side was Rochambeau with French troops, aggregating 8,400 men, and 5,500 Continental troops under Washington, together with 3,000 militia, who were of less account. Against this military and naval force, Cornwallis had 7,500 men within the works of Yorktown, exclusive of 800 marines, disembarked from some English frigate which had lain in the river. Under these circumstances the surrender of the English force was plainly a mere question of time. It may be said, however, that the presence of the land force at a place where it could so happily co operate with the French fleet, bears witness to great strategical ability, and it has been usual to give the credit of the combination to Washington. It is clear, however, that throughout the summer of 1781, the American commander had not seriously contemplated anything but a concerted attack on Sir Henry Clinton in New York. From the day, however, that De Grasse arrived in the Chesapeake, and notified the American and French commanders that he would take his ships no further northward, it required no great strategist to perceive that the land forces must operate in Virginia, if at all. From that moment the objective point of Washington and Rochambeau was palpably the force which Cornwallis, in obedience to Clinton's orders, had collected at Yorktown. Cornwallis, on his part, because he counted, tified in remaining on the peninsula, before, nor afterward, English fleet, and neither then, nor possible that an Admiral any Englishman have supposed it controlled would have acknowledged himself beaten on the sea by Frenchmen till half of his ships were sunk.

In view of these facts, it behooves us in this great celebration at Yorktown, to render our French visitors the honors they deserve, for the event commemorated is more truly and emphatically a French than an American achievement.

The October 1781 issue of the Colonial Gazette *ran Washington's triumphant letter announcing Cornwallis's surrender. The newspaper also hailed the invaluable contributions made by French troops.*

incredible depth and diversity of his knowledge. Among other things, he described the mountains, plants, animals, forests, climate, history, laws, and customs of his native state.

In the book, Jefferson also offered several of his ideas and opinions on political philosophy. For instance, he explained why it is important not to put too much power in the hands of any one branch of government. It is not just the head of state who might abuse his position. Even a legislature elected by the people, he said, could become corrupt. "One hundred and seventy-three despots would surely be as oppressive as one," he wrote. The people, Jefferson warned, must provide for a balance of power among the legislature, the head of state, and the courts. Otherwise, one branch will surely accumulate too much money and power. Jefferson wrote:

The public money and liberty intended to have been deposited with three branches of magistracy [government], but found inadvertently to be in the hands of one only, will soon be discovered to be sources of wealth and dominion [power] to those who hold them. . . . Nor should our assembly be deluded [fooled] by the integrity of their own purposes [their good intentions], and conclude that these unlimited powers will never be abused, because [they] themselves are not disposed [do not intend] to abuse them. They should look forward to a time, and that not a distant one, when a corruption . . . will have seized the head of government. . . . Human nature is the same on every side of the Atlantic, and will be alike influenced by the same causes. The time to guard against corruption and tyranny, is before they shall have gotten hold of us. It is better to keep the wolf out of the fold, than to trust to drawing [out] his teeth and claws after he shall have entered.[33]

Because of his expression of these and other similar ideas, many well-known European writers and philosophers praised Jefferson. He became the chief American contributor to the Enlightenment, a movement among intellectuals of the 1700s and 1800s that stressed the importance of human reason, of scientific logic, and of forming governments free of tyranny.

It was also during this pause from public affairs that Jefferson suffered one of the greatest tragedies of his life. His wife, Martha, then thirty-four, had been ill since the birth of their sixth child a few months before. Her health worsened steadily until September 6, 1782. On that day, Jefferson recorded in his journal, called the Account Book, "My dear wife died this day at 11:45 A.M."[34] He was devastated. For the next several weeks, he could not work or receive visitors. In a state of deep depression, Jefferson paced his library all through the day and night, sleeping only after collapsing from exhaustion. When he finally began leaving the house, he rode his horse for hours through the lonely trails of the surrounding forests. Jefferson, only thirty-nine, had become a widower with three children. (The other three died during infancy.) In addition to Martha, whom he called Patsy, two other daughters—Mary and Lucy—survived their mother.

The Death of Martha

When his wife, Martha, died on September 6, 1782, Jefferson was overwhelmed with grief. The following account of his reactions on that fateful day were recorded by his eldest daughter, also named Martha but whom he called Patsy, some forty years later. His granddaughter, Sarah Randolph, later quoted Patsy in her book The Domestic Life of Thomas Jefferson:

"A moment before the closing scene [death], [my father] was led from the room almost in a state of insensibility by his sister Mrs. Carr who with great difficulty got him into his library where he fainted and remained so long insensible that they feared he never would revive. The scene that followed I did not witness but the violence of his emotion, of his grief when almost by stealth I entered his room at night to this day I dare not trust myself to describe. He kept [stayed in] his room for almost three weeks and I was never a moment from his side. He walked almost incessantly night and day only lying down occasionally when nature was completely exhausted on a pallet [straw-filled mattress] that he had brought in during his long fainting fit. My aunts remained constantly with him for some weeks. I do not remember how many. When at last he left his room he rode out and from that time [on] he was incessantly on horseback rambling about the mountain in the least frequented roads and just as often through the woods; in those melancholy [emotional] rambles I was his constant companion, a solitary witness to many a violent burst of grief, the remembrance of which has consecrated [made special and memorable] particular scenes of that lost home beyond the power of time to obliterate."

Jefferson's eldest daughter (left), named Martha after her mother but nicknamed Patsy, told of her father's deep grief over the death of her mother.

54 ■ THE IMPORTANCE OF THOMAS JEFFERSON

Congressman and World Traveler

Perhaps to help distract himself from his depression over the loss of his wife, Jefferson once again began to accept offers to serve the public. Virginia leaders appointed him to represent the state in Congress, which met in Annapolis, Maryland, in 1784. Jefferson was a congressman for only a few months, but in that time, he accomplished more than most lawmakers do in an entire career. First, he addressed the question of what the nation should do about its vast frontier that sprawled westward from the Appalachian Mountains. He proposed a number of new frontier states and even suggested names for them, like Michigania and Illinoia, which later became Michigan and Illinois. He also advocated that slavery be banned from the Northwest Territory, the large area directly south and west of the Great Lakes. Congress did not accept Jefferson's plan in 1784. But his ideas became

Jefferson established a new monetary system for the United States. It was based on the decimal system and consisted of dollars (above), dimes, and pennies.

the basis for the Northwest Ordinance of 1787, which did prohibit slavery in the Northwest Territory.

Jefferson's other lasting achievement as congressman was the establishment of a new monetary system for the United States. Like many Americans, he considered the British system of pounds, farthings, and pence cumbersome and hard to calculate.

Benjamin Franklin (center) attended many gatherings in his job as minister to France. Franklin, Jefferson, and John Adams were all appointed as special envoys to Europe.

Travel Journals

The incredible range of Jefferson's interests and his attention to the smallest details are evident in the travel journals he kept when visiting Europe as the U.S. minister to France. In the following journal entry made in March 1788, he describes the region of western Germany near the towns of Dusseldorf and Cologne:

"From Duysberg to Dusseldorf the road leads sometimes over the hills, sometimes through the plains of the Rhine [river], the quality of which are as before described. On the hills, however, are considerable groves of oak, of spontaneous growth, which seem to be of more than a century [old]; but the soil being barren, the trees, though high, are crooked and knotty. The undergrowth is broom and moss. In the plains is corn entirely. . . . The houses are poor and ruinous [falling apart], mostly of brick, and scantling [timber] mixed. A good deal of grape cultivated. . . . The plains from Dusseldorf to Cologne are much more extensive, and go off in barren downs at some distance from the river. . . . They [the inhabitants] are manuring the plains with lime. . . . We cross at Cologne on a pendulum boat. I observe the hog of this country . . . of which the celebrated ham is made, is tall, gaunt [thin], and with heavy lop ears. Fatted at a year old, would weigh one hundred or one hundred and twenty pounds. . . . Their principal food is acorns. The pork, fresh, sells at two and a half pence sterling [silver] the pound. The hams, ready made, at eight and a half pence sterling the pound. One hundred and six pounds of this country is equal to one hundred pounds of Holland. About four pounds of fine Holland salt is put on one hundred pounds of pork. It is smoked in a room which has no chimney. Well-informed people here tell me there is no other part of the world where the bacon is smoked. They do not know that we do it. . . . They find that the small hog makes the sweetest meat."

Jefferson proposed simpler denominations based on the decimal system. Congress agreed with him, and his dollars, dimes, and pennies became the standard coinage.

Jefferson's representation of Virginia in Congress was distinguished but did not last long. In May 1784, Congress appointed him as a special envoy to negotiate treaties of commerce with various European countries. Benjamin Franklin, at that time minister to France, and John Adams were also appointed. Jefferson took his daughter

Patsy along to visit Paris, which would become his place of residence for the next few years. From there, he visited several nearby countries, including England, the Netherlands, Italy, and Germany. He recorded everything he saw—people and their customs, geography, animals, and plants—in a series of detailed travel journals. He also collected and sent home many of the newest books by European writers. James Madison alone received almost two hundred books from Jefferson during this period, volumes that influenced Madison's work on the U.S. Constitution.

Although Jefferson greatly enjoyed his busy European adventure, he secretly longed for the peaceful solitude of Monticello. But he would not see his home for a long while yet. In May 1785, the aging Benjamin Franklin resigned, and Jefferson became the U.S. minister to France.

King Louis XVI of France resisted calls to reform his nation's rigid monarchy.

Franklin resigned as U.S. minister to France in 1785. Jefferson succeeded him in the post.

The depth of Jefferson's admiration for Franklin was evident when a French diplomat asked him if he was replacing Franklin. "No one can replace him, sir," Jefferson answered. "I am only his successor."[35]

During his four-year stay in France, Jefferson made a strong and lasting impression on French leaders and thinkers. Many French people wanted to remodel their own society, a rigid monarchy, along the lines of the new United States. But Louis XVI, the French king, was not interested in reform. As biographer Henry Moscow explains, Jefferson witnessed the beginnings of unrest in France that would soon lead to bloody revolution:

> When Jefferson arrived in France he renewed his friendship with the Marquis de Lafayette, who had fought with

the colonists in the Revolution. Because of Lafayette's friendship, every door in France opened to him; the wittiest women, the wisest statesmen and scientists competed to [spend time with him]. . . . The French winter of 1788–1789 was a dreadful one. Jefferson recorded temperatures of 18 below zero. . . . The government had to keep great bonfires blazing at Paris street corners to keep people from freezing to death. . . . In these dangerous times the Marquis de Lafayette drew up a Declaration of the Rights of Man—modeled on Jefferson's ideas—and the new National Assembly began writing a Constitution embracing it. [But] Louis, influenced by conservative ministers . . . confronted the people with troops instead of reforms. . . . Jefferson saw the first popular uprisings in Paris which led to the storming of the Bastille [prison], symbol of the government's power.[36]

Arguments About the Nation's Future

As the French Revolution began, Jefferson sailed for home, arriving at Monticello on December 23, 1789. He was home only a few months before his friends James Madison and George Washington, who had been elected president on April 30, 1789, approached him. After a great deal of discussion and pleading, they convinced Jefferson to become the country's first secretary of state. Jefferson's new duties included supervising the nation's foreign affairs and running the U.S. Patent Office.

The most dramatic aspect of Jefferson's term as secretary of state was his rivalry with Alexander Hamilton, the country's first secretary of the Treasury. Jefferson and Hamilton had very different ideas about managing the economy and about the country's future in general. In contrast to Jefferson's notion that small farmers of

France's bloody revolution had its beginnings in the storming of the Bastille.

George Washington was elected as president of the United States in 1789. Washington helped convince Jefferson to serve as secretary of state.

to the new democracy. But he did not foresee the coming of a modern world in which the importance of industry would vastly overshadow that of small farmers.

The biggest disagreement between Jefferson and Hamilton was over how to interpret the nation's new Constitution, which had gone into effect in 1789. According to Jefferson, Congress had no right to establish a national bank because the Constitution did not give it such power. Hamilton argued that Congress had the right to do anything it thought best for the country, as long as the Constitution did not specifically forbid it. President Washington wanted Jefferson and Hamilton to settle their differences and reach an agreement on the matter. But Jefferson, fearing they would never agree, replied: "As to a coalition [agreement] with Mr. Hamilton, if by that was meant that either was to sacrifice his general system to

Alexander Hamilton served as the nation's first secretary of the treasury. He and Jefferson clashed often on economic and constitutional matters.

modest means were the base on which to build the economy, Hamilton championed business and industry. Hamilton wanted to form a National Bank, which would issue paper money and back ventures by merchants and manufacturers. Only with a strong industrial base, he said, could the nation grow and prosper.

In retrospect, neither man was totally right nor totally wrong. Hamilton correctly saw that the economy needed an industrial base. But he did not foresee that this would concentrate a great deal of wealth in the hands of a few rich and powerful industrialists. On the other hand, Jefferson predicted such a concentration of wealth. Seeing it as a return to the old-style aristocracy, Jefferson believed it to be dangerous the other, it was impossible. We had both no doubt formed our conclusions after the most mature consideration; and principles conscientiously adopted could not be given up on either side."[37]

And neither side ever did give up its principles. As Henry Moscow explains:

> The argument between Jefferson and Hamilton about interpretation of the Constitution is an argument which has never been settled in the government of the United States. Jefferson's position represents the "strict" interpretation . . . and Hamilton's position represents the "loose construction." Even today, when Congress considers a new and major bill, there are those senators and congressmen who take Jeffersonian or Hamiltonian positions as to whether or not the Constitution permits the law. It is often the function of the Supreme Court, once laws have left Congress, to make the final decision on whether or not the law is constitutional.[38]

A Threat to American Freedom

The political feud between Jefferson and Hamilton continued until Jefferson, once again longing for home, resigned as secretary of state in July 1793. Washington, who had begun his second term as president, convinced Jefferson to stay on until the end of the year. Finally, in the spring of 1794, the master of Monticello settled down in his hilltop estate for what seemed to him a deserved retirement. He planted twenty-four hundred weeping

John Adams ran for president as a candidate of the Federalist party, and won.

willow blossoms in March and resumed his many interests and activities.

But Jefferson's retirement was doomed by his own great abilities and importance. By now, whether he liked it or not, he was one of the country's leading figures, and many of his former colleagues demanded his services again. In 1796, there was to be an election to replace the retiring George Washington. Madison and other leaders of the new Republican party needed a candidate to run against the Federalist party candidate John Adams. Even though Jefferson said openly that he did not want the job, the Republicans picked him as their candidate.

At the time, as it is today, picking the president and vice-president was the job of the electoral college. Its members, called electors, are special representatives from each state, and they vote on the candidates

Monticello

During the 1790s, while serving as secretary of state and vice-president, Jefferson spent a great deal of time planning revisions for Monticello. In his book Thomas Jefferson and the New Nation, *historian Merrill D. Peterson describes the unique look that Jefferson's architectural genius brought to the project:*

"The house was an ideal: the . . . expression in brick and mortar and wood of a man's capacity to humanize his environment. As an ideal it would never be finished. . . . Planning commenced in 1792, and all was in readiness months before he retired from office. The house as it stood was a two-story center block with shallow wings terminating in octagonal [eight-sided] bays. Porticoes [walkways with roofs supported by columns] adorned both fronts. The entrance hall, stairs on either side, led into a grand salon, or parlor, as Jefferson called it. . . . The dining room was in the wing to the right, the drawing room and master's quarters in the wing to the left. His library was nicely accommodated in the spacious quarters above the parlor. . . . According to the master plan of 1792, the basement was to connect at either end with long L-shaped wings sunk into the northern and southern slopes and covered with terraces on a level with the main floor of the house. . . . Only one change was proposed in the west front, the addition of a dome, but it was the crowning touch. . . . Such was the new Monticello. The plan was not matured all at once, but it was fully embodied in a drawing Jefferson made in 1796. As the work progressed he figured the specifications down to the last detail. In a notebook kept for this purpose are sketches . . . and builder's directions for cornices, columns, dome . . . fireplaces, mantles, chimneys, windows, curtains, and so on. The house would thus become an unrivaled, and quite inexhaustible, statement of his own personality. It had no prototype. . . . It had an architectural integrity [look and style] wholly its own, and so can only be described as Jeffersonian."

Jefferson renovated Monticello throughout his life.

for president and vice-president nominated by each party. The difference in Jefferson's day was that of the four men, regardless of party, the person who received the most votes became president and the person who came in second became vice-president. The final election tally, announced in February 1797, were seventy-one votes for Adams and sixty-eight votes for Jefferson. Jefferson was now a Republican vice-president under a Federalist president. He was more than a little reluctant, but out of a sense of duty to his country, Jefferson accepted the job.

Jefferson spent much of his time as vice-president opposing the Alien and Sedition Acts. The Alien Act empowered the president to deport any noncitizen whom he considered dangerous to the nation's security. The Sedition Act made it a federal offense to criticize the government, the Congress, or the president. These laws were passed in 1797 after a series of diplomatic disputes with France resulted in anti-French feeling sweeping the United States. The Federalists, fearing that war with France was imminent, urged Congress to pass the Alien and Sedition Acts to prevent foreign "agitators" from disrupting the nation. Many Federalists feared that French citizens and other foreign visitors might influence Americans to turn on their own government. In reality, however, the acts were used against other Americans, including Republicans. Ten Republican printers who published anti-Federalist literature were arrested, tried, and convicted under the Sedition Act. Some outraged Republicans called the laws part of a Federalist "reign of terror."

Jefferson agreed. He pointed out one provision of the Alien Act designed to discourage Americans and foreigners from mingling and exchanging views. The provision required him to send a messenger seventy miles for written permission from a federal judge before having a foreign guest visit Monticello. Both laws, he said, were undemocratic and unconstitutional. They denied citizens their right of free speech and association guaranteed by the Constitution. Although he was Adams's vice-president, Jefferson was also the leader of the opposition party. He was the natural choice to lead the fight against the new laws.

Jefferson did not succeed in overturning the Alien and Sedition Acts while vice-president, mainly because the Republicans lacked the votes in Congress. But the battle over the laws would soon have important consequences. The bitter fight against what he saw as a new form of tyranny made Jefferson view the Federalists as a threat to American freedom. "The philosopher of Monticello," said Roger Bruns, "the gentleman farmer, the man who despised much of the political environment, was now determined to put his heart and genius into ousting the Federalists from power. Virginia's famous man of letters and learning was also a crafty political organizer. He geared up to take on John Adams [in the next election]. This time it would not be as a reluctant candidate, but as an eager, driven one."[39]

5 Reaching for New Horizons

After a tough, uphill election fight, Thomas Jefferson became the third president of the United States. His major goal was to weaken the Federalist hold on the government and on the nation. He believed that they were leading the country in the wrong direction and trampling many personal freedoms. Federalist leaders like Adams and Hamilton meant well, Jefferson felt, but they put too much power in the hands of a few wealthy and influential men. Jefferson wanted to reaffirm the democratic ideals and goals that the patriots had fought for in the Revolution. He believed this was necessary for the country's survival.

A Moving Speech Ends a Bitter Campaign

The election campaign of 1800 was hard-fought and bitter. The Republicans picked New York legislator Aaron Burr to run as Jefferson's vice-presidential candidate. John Adams, running for a second term, led the Federalist ticket. His running mate was a popular politician from South Carolina named Charles C. Pinckney. Disagreements and rivalries between the two political parties led to angry name-calling and dirty politics, particularly on the part of the

Federalists. Trying to keep the Republicans from gaining power, Federalist writers and speakers accused Jefferson of being a godless atheist who would drag the country into an orgy of crime and sin. Backing the Federalists, a newspaper called the *Gazette of the*

Aaron Burr ran as Jefferson's vice-presidential candidate in Jefferson's second campaign for president.

Dirty Campaign Tactics

Accustomed to the smear tactics and negative campaigning used in modern television ads during presidential elections, people tend to forget that many of the campaigns of previous centuries were just as mean-spirited. The fight between the Republicans and the Federalists in 1800 was an example. In his essay "Thomas Jefferson: A Brief Life," Merrill D. Peterson recounts:

"The election of 1800 was unusually bitter. Around the person of Jefferson the Republicans achieved a unity of action and feeling not known before. He was presented to the public as 'the man of the people,' while Adams was draped in the hideous garments of kings and nobles. The Federalists, sharply divided among themselves, united in sounding [a warning] about Jefferson, vilifying [denouncing] him as a Jacobin incendiary [warlike Frenchman], infidel [atheist], visionary [dreamer] . . . , and the enemy of Washington, the Constitution, and the Union. For ten years Federalist pundits had been fashioning this ugly image of Jefferson. Now it became a diabolical obsession. Under him, surely, the churches would be destroyed and the nation laid waste by revolutionary fanaticism imported from France. 'Murder, robbery, rape, adultery, and incest will be openly taught and practiced,' wrote one pamphleteer [campaign writer], 'the air will be rent with the cries of distress, and the soil will be soaked with blood, and the nation black with crimes.' Jefferson, while personally hurt by the smear campaign, nursed his wounds in private. He had long since learned that for every libel [insulting lie] put down another rose in its place; besides, he was committed philosophically to the widest latitude of public discussion on the principle he would state in his Inaugural Address: 'that error of opinion may be tolerated where reason is left free to combat it.'"

United States stated, "At the present solemn moment the only question to be asked by every American, laying his hand on his heart, is 'Shall I continue in allegiance to GOD—AND A RELIGIOUS PRESIDENT; or impiously declare for JEFFERSON—AND NO GOD!!!'"[40] And Alexander Hamilton, still Jefferson's staunchest political foe,

spoke openly about keeping that "atheist in religion . . . from getting possession of the helm of state."[41]

The Federalists also branded Jefferson a coward for running from Tarleton's troops at Monticello during the Revolution. For months, Jefferson, who had proved himself an honest and model citizen time and again,

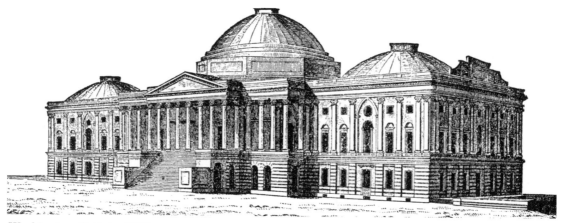
Washington, D.C. in 1800.

suffered a barrage of insults as his opponents called him a thief, scoundrel, and ruffian. But he refused to stoop to such underhanded tactics himself. During the campaign, he remained in solitude at Monticello and made no public speeches.

In November 1800, Jefferson traveled to Washington, D.C., which had become the nation's new capital the preceding June. There, in what was still a small village bordered by swamps, he awaited the results of the electors' vote. His victory over Adams and Pinckney did not surprise him, for he had expected to defeat the Federalists. But he had not expected his own running mate to do so well. The vote was seventy-three for Jefferson, seventy-three for Burr, sixty-five for Adams, and sixty-four for Pinckney. Because of the tie between Jefferson and Burr, it was up to the House of Representatives to choose the president. After nineteen separate ballots, in which each congressman voted for the person he felt would most help the country, the House picked Jefferson.

At about noon on March 4, 1801, the fifty-seven-year-old Jefferson, dressed plainly, strode up New Jersey Avenue to the Capitol to be inaugurated. Apart from the traditional firing of cannons, the ceremony was simple. Aaron Burr, the new vice-president,

Jefferson arrives in the nation's capital to await election results. He was inaugurated as the third U.S. president in March 1801.

sat on Jefferson's right. John Marshall, the new chief justice of the Supreme Court, who would administer the oath of office, sat on his left.

Though he did not normally like being in the public spotlight, Jefferson thoroughly enjoyed this public moment of triumph. He delivered a magnificent speech, calling for members of the two parties to unite in the common cause of freedom. He said:

> To you . . . gentlemen who are charged with the sovereign functions of legislation . . . I look with encouragement for the guidance and support which may enable us to steer with safety the vessel [nation] in which we are all embarked amid the conflicting elements of a troubled world. . . . We are all republicans—we are all federalists. If there be any among us who would wish to dissolve this Union or to change its republican [democratic] form, let them stand undisturbed as monuments of the safety with which error of opinion may be tolerated where reason is left free to combat it.

Jefferson also set forth the principles of government he felt were most important and which he would pursue as president:

> About to enter, fellow citizens, on the exercise of duties which comprehend everything dear and valuable to you, it is proper that you should understand what I deem the essential principles of our government, and consequently those which ought to shape its administration. . . . Equal and exact justice to all men, of whatever state or persuasion, religious or political; peace, commerce, and honest friendship with all nations . . . freedom of religion; freedom of the press; freedom of person.[42]

After the audience acknowledged the speech with a thunderous ovation, Jefferson received the oath of office from Justice Marshall. It was one of the high points of Jefferson's life. Yet the joy and pride he felt at that moment were tempered by a note of sadness. His beloved wife had not lived to see him become leader of the nation he had helped found. And his old friend John Adams, embittered by the hard campaign and lost election, had shunned the ceremony. Jefferson hoped that eventually they would be able to renew their friendship.

Assault on the Opposition

Despite his call for unity between the two political parties, Jefferson still saw the Federalists as a threat. So he sought to repeal or change every Federalist policy and custom he could. His first order of business as president, for example, was to bring the theme of simplicity so evident at his inauguration into the everyday affairs of his office. Washington and Adams, both staunch Federalists, had run their presidencies with a great deal of formality and ceremony. Jefferson rejected this kind of pomp, feeling that it was an obnoxious leftover from the days of the British monarchy. He wanted to eliminate, he said, "all those public forms and ceremonies which tended to familiarize the public eye to the harbingers [forerunners] of another [and less democratic] form of government."[43] So that people would see the president as modest and unassuming, Jefferson forbade the use of his face on coins and refused to let the country celebrate his birthday. Also, said Irwin Unger:

In place of his predecessors' regal ceremonial visits to Congress to express their wishes on matters of new legislation or policy, Jefferson substituted written messages. Instead of "levees," stiff, formal occasions at which members of the government and . . . diplomats paid court to the president in strict order of rank, Jefferson gave state dinners at which guests took whatever seat they could find. Many affairs of the executive mansion, moreover, were open to the public, and many people took advantage of the opportunity to rub shoulders with the great. . . . Still more characteristic of Jefferson were the small dinners, with guests seated at a round table where no one could claim precedence [importance] over anyone else. The president held these informal gatherings dressed in carpet slippers and a threadbare scarlet vest, his shirt not always perfectly clean. The guests discussed philosophy, the arts, literature, and science while eating food served by the president himself.[44]

In addition to eliminating most of the Federalists' formal customs, Jefferson also reversed the effects of much of their legislation. First, he pardoned every person imprisoned under the Sedition Act and even wrote them letters of apology for what the government had put them through. Spurred on by Jefferson, the Republican majority in Congress repealed the Alien and Sedition Acts. Foreign visitors were no longer under suspicion. Jefferson also eliminated Hamilton's national bank and several heavy Federalist-imposed taxes. So vigorous was his attack on the Federalists, their ideas, and their policies that they never again regained their former power and influence.

The Scandal That Would Not Go Away

Nevertheless, though their power had been diminished, the Federalists continued to oppose Jefferson. Periodically, Federalist writers slandered or tried to discredit him, as they had during the campaign. Few people paid much attention to these attacks, considering that they came from the bitter opposition.

When a scandalous attack came from one of the president's own former followers, however, more people took notice. In 1802, James T. Callender, who had written anti-Federalist pamphlets for the Republicans in the late 1790s, accused Jefferson of having a love affair with Sally Hemmings, one of Jefferson's slaves. According to Callender, Hemmings had five children by Jefferson, one of whom ended up in a New Orleans slave market with Jefferson's consent. The Federalists, ever eager to make Jefferson look bad, quickly tried to capitalize on the accusation. Several newspapers sympathetic to the Federalists printed the charge, and Jefferson's enemies used it against him in the next election. Some papers even published cruel poems about Jefferson and Hemmings. Jefferson was furious at these attacks, but he chose not to dignify the charge by speaking of it publicly and denied it only in private. He hoped people would eventually forget about it, but many did not. The charge resurfaced time and again, even when he was an old man.

And the controversy still rages. A few modern historians, including Fawn Brodie and Barbara Chase-Riboud, have supported Callender's accusation. "If the story of the Sally Hemmings liaison [affair] be true, as I believe it is," wrote Brodie in her best-selling book *Thomas Jefferson: An Intimate History,* "it represents . . . a serious passion that brought Jefferson and the slave woman much private happiness over a period lasting thirty-eight years."[45]

Most historians, however, reject this theory. They consider Callender an outright liar. They point out that he had been imprisoned under the Sedition Act, then pardoned by Jefferson. As a reward for his suffering, Callender wanted a government job but Jefferson, who did not like him personally, refused. "Callender began thereupon to make threatening noises," said Pulitzer Prize-winning historian Virginius Dabney, who believes Callender made the charge out of spite.[46] Merrill Peterson agrees. "Like most legends," he wrote, "this one was not created out of the whole cloth. The evidence, highly circumstantial, is far from conclusive."[47]

A Stupendous Bargain

Had Jefferson been a weak president who accomplished little, the scandal unleashed by Callender might have hurt him a great deal more. But Jefferson's many achievements made these and other insulting accusations seem trivial to most Americans. In fact, less than a year after the Sally Hemmings charge surfaced, one of Jefferson's greatest accomplishments earned him the admiration of nearly all Americans and temporarily silenced his critics.

Jefferson had always been fascinated by what lay beyond the western horizon. Now, as president, he turned his attention to the frontier lands west of the Appalachians. He reasoned that his nation of small farmers would one day spread out and settle all of the territory to the east of the mighty Mississippi River. But what of the territory beyond the Mississippi, the area known as Louisiana? This huge expanse of forests, swamps, wide plains, and roving Indian tribes was still largely uncharted and mysterious. Jefferson wondered whether the urge to spread farther west into these unknown lands might eventually prove irresistible to American settlers. That event seemed to lie far in the future, however. Early in 1802, easy access to the Mississippi for Americans living on the frontier was the main concern in the region. The river was the easiest and cheapest way for farmers and trappers to transport their goods to outside markets. Spain owned Louisiana and allowed the United States access to the river through its port of New Orleans at the mouth of the river.

But later that year, this situation abruptly changed. On October 15, 1802, Spain ceded Louisiana to France, at the time ruled by the military dictator Napoleon Bonaparte. In the words of historian James Truslow Adams, "At the stroke of a pen the entire American position was altered. One of the strongest powers in the world, headed by a ruthless and colossally ambitious despot . . . controlled the mouth of the Mississippi." Many Americans, including Jefferson, were worried that France might close the Mississippi, the vital trade route to the frontier. There were also fears that Napoleon would try to establish a new French empire on the American continent.

In order to assure continued U.S. access to the Mississippi, Jefferson decided early in 1803 to try buying New Orleans from France. Luckily, Napoleon was preoccupied by a war with Great Britain at the time. As James Truslow Adams went on to explain:

The Louisiana Purchase

One of the great achievements of Jefferson's presidency was the acquisition of Louisiana, a vast territory west of the Mississippi River. This land nearly doubled the size of the United States and made rapid westward expansion of the country not only possible but also inevitable. Yet Jefferson did not originally plan to buy so huge a tract. At first, his intention was to purchase only New Orleans, as Jefferson's biographer Clara Ingram Judson explained:

"Jefferson thought often about the West, especially that vast part called Louisiana. Most Americans were busy earning a living and had little interest in that part of the country—except perhaps in the Mississippi River. That was the highway to market for hundreds of enterprising settlers. Even they felt little concern about the government of Louisiana. Spain owned it, and she was too weak to make trouble. During his first year in the White House, Jefferson heard that Spain had secretly given Louisiana to Napoleon. That changed the situation. . . . [A] letter was written—an amazing document in which Jefferson daringly threatened the great Napoleon. He also asked for the purchase price of New Orleans. Some time later, news that France owned New Orleans burst upon Americans. Letters poured onto Jefferson's desk.

'Are American crops to float into the arms of France?' . . .

'Settlers won't go west now—that's sure!' . . .

But the president was acting boldly, though quietly. He asked Congress to appropriate two million dollars for international use. Then he sent James Monroe to France to help [Minister to France Robert] Livingston buy New Orleans. These were daring and unprecedented actions. While Monroe was on the ocean, Napoleon was taking stock of his military equipment; he needed more, but lacked the cash. He sent his minister of foreign affairs to talk with Livingston.

'How much will you pay for Louisiana?' the minister asked.

'We had not considered that!' Livingston was dismayed.

'You'd better buy while you can.' . . .

Soon arrangements were settled for the United States to buy Louisiana from France. The cost was about fifteen million dollars. . . . France made a colorful ceremony of the actual transfer [of ownership] at New Orleans on December 20th, 1803."

European affairs had not gone as Napoleon had hoped. . . . His hands were . . . tied by war in the Old World, and he could [not] afford . . . to dream of an empire in America. . . . He suddenly began to think of selling Louisiana to the United States. . . . It would at once relieve him of a drain on his military resources and give him much-needed cash. Jefferson's instructions to his envoys had contemplated no such contingency. They had been [told] to offer fifty million francs for New Orleans. . . . Suddenly . . . [they were] amazed to be asked point-blank what the United States would pay for the whole of Louisiana. . . . The envoys finally bought Louisiana for approximately $15,000,000, giving [the United States] the whole of the Mississippi River and increasing [its] territory from 900,000 square miles to 1,800,000. It was, perhaps, the most stupendous bargain in history.[48]

Jefferson signs the papers consummating the sale. The vast lands of the Louisiana Purchase instantly doubled the size of the United States.

Americans feared that when Napoleon (below) took control of Louisiana he would cut off access to the Mississippi River. Instead, the French ruler sold Louisiana to the United States.

Toward the Far Horizon

Jefferson's huge surprise land deal, popularly referred to as the Louisiana Purchase, became official on May 2, 1803. It instantly doubled the size of the United States. Most Americans, including Jefferson, were awed by the prospects of this incredible deal. At the time, it seemed as though American settlers would have ample room for expansion as well as nearly unlimited natural resources for centuries to come. But exactly what was the extent of these lands and resources? What barriers and pitfalls awaited the first waves of settlers? How many Indians inhabited the area? No one knew for sure. A large landowner in his own right, Jefferson realized that acquiring land was one thing and utilizing it another. Before the new territory could be settled and developed, it had to be

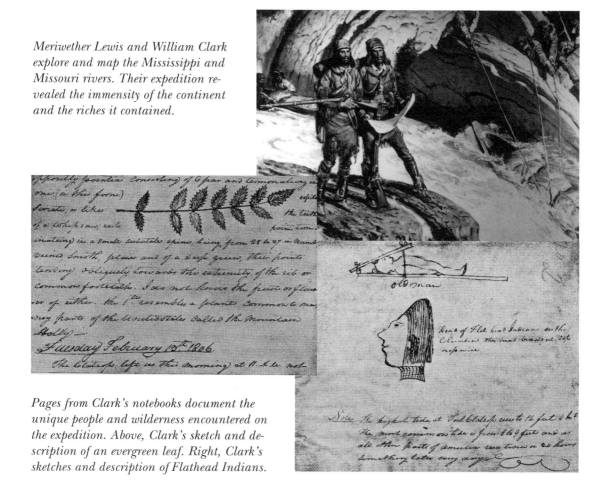

Meriwether Lewis and William Clark explore and map the Mississippi and Missouri rivers. Their expedition revealed the immensity of the continent and the riches it contained.

Pages from Clark's notebooks document the unique people and wilderness encountered on the expedition. Above, Clark's sketch and description of an evergreen leaf. Right, Clark's sketches and description of Flathead Indians.

explored and mapped. "An intelligent officer," he proposed, "with ten or twelve chosen men . . . might explore the whole line, even to the Western Ocean" and return with priceless information.[49]

Immediately after Louisiana was in American hands, Jefferson began planning the venture he had dreamed about since boyhood—a journey toward the far horizon to unlock the secrets of unknown lands. Jefferson chose his close friend and secretary, Meriwether Lewis, to lead the expedition. Lewis asked that his old army friend Capt. William Clark be allowed to

share command and Jefferson agreed. "The object of your mission," Jefferson told Lewis, "is . . . the direct water communication from sea to sea formed by the bed of the Missouri [River] and perhaps the Oregon. . . . I have proposed . . . that Congress shall appropriate ten or twelve thousand dollars for exploring the principal waters of the Mississippi and Missouri."[50] Jefferson ordered Lewis to observe and record his position on maps each day with "great precision and accuracy" and also to gather information on the various Indian tribes encountered along the way. In addition,

The Lewis and Clark Expedition

Jefferson saw clearly that after acquiring the vast lands of the Louisiana Purchase, the next logical step was to explore and map these lands. Jefferson organized the Lewis and Clark expedition. He also sponsored several other explorations, according to Pulitzer Prize-winning historian William Goetzmann in his essay "Savage Enough to Prefer the Woods: The Cosmopolite and the West":

" The significance of the Lewis and Clark expedition overshadowed even their epic wilderness achievement. Besides the incredible amount of scientific data they brought back, including Indian artifacts, animal skins and scientific specimens enough to fill Peale's entire museum in Philadelphia, they had gained a sense of the immensity of the continent and of the riches it contained. In looking for a Northwest Passage—which they did not find—Lewis and Clark had discovered the vast interior of North America and dramatized its potential for the new American republic. While European nations struggled half-heartedly and clumsily for control of North America, Lewis and Clark made it possible, indeed virtually inevitable, that citizens of the United States should take possession of it. They more than fulfilled . . . Jefferson's continental dream. Understandably enough, the idea of the West so gripped Jefferson that he did not rest content with the achievement of Lewis and Clark's expedition. He also sent William Dunbar and John Hunter west in 1804 to explore the Red River and other southern tributaries of the Mississippi so as to chart the limits of his Louisiana Purchase. . . . And for a time he allowed . . . [the] military governor of Louisiana to send out expeditions under Zebulon Pike to the sources of the Mississippi and to the headwaters of the Arkansas. . . . The years of Jefferson's presidency were years of intense government and private fur trader exploring activity. . . . William Clark, soon established in St. Louis as the new Governor of Louisiana, continually collected every bit of information he could from trappers, traders, Indians and official explorers for incorporation into his master map of the West."

Lewis and Clark and their team of explorers encountered severe hardships on their journey. But the information they brought home with them would prove invaluable to Americans as they moved west.

the members of the expedition were to accurately record "the soil and the face of the country . . . the animals . . . the remains [of prehistoric beasts] . . . the mineral productions of every kind . . . volcanic appearances . . . climate . . . the dates at which particular plants put forth or lose their flowers, or leaf, times of appearance of particular birds, reptiles or insects."[51]

In May 1804, Lewis and Clark began their legendary journey by guiding three boats crammed with men and supplies down the Missouri River. During the next two years, the expedition encountered numerous severe hardships, including sickness, bad weather, overturned boats, attacks by grizzly bears and rattlesnakes, inadequate food, and deadly river rapids.

In September 1806, after traveling more than eight thousand miles, the explorers returned to Saint Louis. No one had heard from them the whole time and many, including Jefferson, feared they might be dead. Hearing of their safe return, Jefferson expressed "unspeakable joy." Despite its hardships, the expedition had been an unqualified success. The explorers brought back a vast store of information that would prove invaluable to American settlers and developers. But seeing the excitement and fascination the expedition generated across the country, Jefferson realized that the men had done much more than just gather information. They had ignited a spark in the minds and hearts of millions of people. They had opened a door to lands of adventure and opportunity, untamed lands that beckoned to those with the courage to tame them. "The importance of the Lewis and Clark expedition," remarked historian Henry Nash Smith, "lay on the level of imagination: it was drama, it was the enactment of a myth that embodied the future."[52]

In less than three years, Thomas Jefferson had done more to shape that future than Washington and Adams combined. Jefferson had brought the nation untold riches in land and natural resources and an immense potential for growth. In the decades to come, millions of Americans would exploit that potential, helping transform the United States into a prosperous and powerful nation. Had all of Jefferson's other magnificent accomplishments never existed, this single achievement would have been enough to ensure him immortality.

6 Struggle for Peace

Jefferson had vowed in 1801 that he would serve only one term as president, then retire to Monticello. But by 1804, he was comfortable in the job. Moreover, he felt he had not completed some of the tasks he had set out to accomplish. He had been successful in dismantling many of the Federalist laws and policies he saw as dangerous to freedom. But other Federalist policies and customs lingered, and the Federalists were still determined to regain the presidency. Jefferson felt the country was still in danger of slipping backward and losing some of the democratic ideals he held dear. The nation still needed him, he believed, so he decided to run for a second term.

During his second term, however, Jefferson found himself preoccupied mainly with foreign affairs and national defense. Great Britain and France, who had fought each other off and on for decades, clashed again. This time, by kidnapping American sailors and firing on American ships, they threatened to drag the United States into the conflict. To make matters worse, tensions between Britain and the United States had been growing steadily for years. Since the Revolution, the two countries had become bitter trade rivals. Also, the British were still angry over losing their American colonies, and the Americans still

viewed British leaders as arrogant and tyrannical. In a series of controversial incidents at sea, each side felt it had been provoked. The threat of war loomed often.

During these years, Jefferson strove constantly to keep the United States from going to war. This was partly because he was a pacifist at heart. "Peace is my passion," he remarked on many occasions. He believed that fighting was useless and that war should be a last resort. Jefferson also hoped that the United States might avoid the destructive wars that had ravaged Europe for centuries. He hoped that because the country was isolated from Europe, it would enjoy peace and prosperity. In any case, he knew that Britain and France were much more powerful than the United States. A war with either of these countries might be disastrous, resulting in a loss of everything the Americans had gained since the Revolution. During Jefferson's second term, he struggled to maintain peace. Despite gallant efforts, it was a struggle he would lose.

A Loss of Public Confidence

At least one aspect of Jefferson's second term—regaining the presidency—involved

Impressment Leads to War

One of the worst crises of Jefferson's second term as president occurred in June 1807. It became one of a series of incidents that eventually led to the War of 1812. The British had reason to believe that a British deserter named Jenkin Ratford, who had publicly criticized his own countrymen, was aboard an American ship. Historian James Truslow Adams, in The Living Jefferson, *describes the encounter between the British and the Americans:*

"The American ship of war *Chesapeake* sailed from Hampton Roads [Virginia], not quite ready for sea, due to delays in fitting her out. Some miles off the coast she was ordered to stop by the British ship *Leopard,* whose captain demanded the right to search her for British subjects. British commanders had stopped American merchant vessels but this was the first time they had dared to stop one belonging to the American navy. On the refusal of the American commander to allow his ship to be searched, the British opened fire on her, killing or wounding twenty . . . men. In view of the unprepared condition of the *Chesapeake,* she was unable to fight and had to surrender and yield to search. Three sailors, two Americans and one British deserter [Ratford], though his presence had been unknown to the [U.S.] commander, [James] Barron, were taken off. A howl of rage went up from America, and Jefferson by a word could have had war against England. He held the situation [showed restraint], however, in spite of being accused of . . . [cowardice]. He issued a proclamation forbidding British war vessels to enter American waters, and prohibiting all intercourse with them."

no struggle at all. Unlike the closely contested race in 1800, the election of 1804 resulted in a landslide victory for Jefferson. He won the support of the electors of nearly every state, defeating the Federalist candidate, Charles C. Pinckney, by 162 votes to 14. Few people were surprised. Jefferson's first term had been very successful overall, and his popularity soared. Even some of his regular critics, like influential congressman John Randolph of Virginia, admitted the scope of his accomplishments.

Remarked Randolph, "Never was there an administration more brilliant . . . taxes repealed: the public debt amply provided for . . . Louisiana acquired; public confidence unbounded."[53]

But this widespread confidence did not last long. Jefferson had dealt effectively with the largely domestic issues of his first term, issues over which he had at least some measure of control. But after 1804, nearly all of the problems he faced were foreign policy issues. He could not predict or control the whims and actions of other countries. Therefore, his policies became increasingly less successful and less popular with the American people. The frustrated Jefferson came to appreciate George Washington's warning that the United States should avoid "foreign entanglements."

The ongoing hostilities between Britain and France were Jefferson's biggest foreign problem. Napoleon was preparing his forces for a major invasion of Britain. French ships challenged Britain's navy, the largest in the world, and each side claimed the right to seize any foreign ships daring to deal with its enemy. This put the United States, the world's largest neutral trading nation, in a difficult position. The country needed trade with at least one of these wealthy nations to maintain a healthy economy. But no matter which side it dealt with, it would risk losing ships and sailors. Merrill Peterson explained the dilemma Jefferson faced:

> It was ironic that the President who put a continent at the feet of his countrymen . . . [who rejected] the wars and intrigues of European politics . . . should have found himself embroiled [involved] during his second term in a struggle for American rights on the high seas. . . . Each side [Britain and France] demanded [U.S.] trade on its own terms; adherence to one entailed conflict with the other. While Jefferson might try to play off one power against the other . . . neither feared war with the United States, whose President prided himself on peace . . . and who had neither army nor navy to speak of. So both Britain and France played fast and loose with American neutrality.[54]

Rising Tensions on the High Seas

The situation worsened when the British began seizing American ships with the express purpose of impressing, or forcing into service, American sailors. The British had lost many of their own sailors to battle

A British naval officer orders an American sailor into service for the British navy. This practice outraged Americans, leading many to urge a declaration of war.

and desertion and tried to fill the ranks with captured Americans. People across the United States expressed outrage, and many demanded that Jefferson declare war. But he wanted desperately to keep the nation out of a European conflict, especially with Britain. The British, he knew, would like nothing better than to retake their lost colonies by force. Jefferson also realized that the Americans were no match for the British on the seas. The British had more than six hundred warships, and more than two hundred of those carried over forty cannons. By contrast, the United States had fewer than twenty warships, and only seven carried more than thirty cannons. Jefferson believed it was foolhardy to risk a war the country was not prepared to fight.

But as tensions between the United States and Europe continued to increase, so did the American public's demands for war. The British and the French placed increasingly outrageous restrictions on the United States, making Jefferson's peaceful stance more difficult to maintain. According to Irwin Unger:

> In May 1806 Britain announced a blockade of the European continent. . . . Napoleon responded with the Berlin Decree, placing Britain under blockade and forbidding all British commerce with France. Any vessel [including American ships] coming from Britain or attempting to penetrate the blockade would be seized. Now it was Britain's turn. In 1807 the British issued two orders in council threatening to confiscate all ships engaged in French coastal trade. . . . Only if they first stopped in Britain, paid duties, and secured British clearance would neutrals be allowed to

Britain and America came perilously close to war when a British navy vessel opened fire on the American warship, the Chesapeake, *after its captain refused permission to board.*

> trade with any part of Europe. . . . The British-French war of regulations seemed designed to produce the maximum amount of irritation in America. If American merchants bowed to the British they would offend the French, and vice versa.[55]

The British demands and continued seizures of American sailors caused widespread anti-British feelings among Americans. But these insults were only the beginning. In June 1807, the British warship *Leopard* encountered the American warship *Chesapeake* off the coast of Virginia. Suspecting there was a British deserter aboard the *Chesapeake,* the captain of the *Leopard* demanded the right to board and search the American ship. When the American captain refused, the *Leopard* opened fire, heavily damaging the unprepared *Chesapeake.* The British then boarded the ship, did indeed find their deserter, and in

The British remove a deserter and two American sailors from the damaged Chesapeake. *The incident put added pressure on Jefferson to declare war, but he resisted.*

the process, seized two American sailors. Many Americans felt this outrage should not be tolerated. War fever gripped the United States, and the most militant members of Congress, known popularly as the war hawks, demanded that Jefferson declare war.

Defense or Offense?

But Jefferson once more showed restraint. He issued an order barring British ships from American coastal waters and sent an ambassador to negotiate a settlement. These steps did nothing to stop further British outrages. Many U.S. politicians and newspaper editors charged that Jefferson was too soft on the British, and some even accused him

of cowardice. Under increasing pressure, Jefferson considered other measures.

First, despite his avowed distaste for war, Jefferson proposed beefing up the nation's military. His approach, however, was a cautious one. He felt that building a massive offensive force to match those of Britain and France would take many years, if it could be done at all. So he chose instead to increase the nation's defensive capabilities. He proposed a fleet of 240 gunboats, small war vessels equipped with between one and five cannons, to defend U.S. harbors. But most lawmakers, including many Republicans, rejected this idea as inadequate. They urged building a large navy and new coastal forts instead.

Jefferson was insulted and angry when Congress approved the building of only twenty-five gunboats. "Is it their interest," he asked, "to scout [reject] a defence by gunboats in which they would share amply, in hopes of a navy which will not be built in our day, & would be no defence if built, or of forts which will never be built or maintained, and would be no defence if built?"[56] Jefferson also proposed using submarines equipped with underwater torpedoes to repel invading British ships. Lawmakers found this idea, clearly far ahead of its

An Inventive Military Strategist

As tensions between the United States and Great Britain mounted during Jefferson's second term, he hoped that war could be avoided. But he also recognized that if war came, his country had to be ready to defend itself. So he ordered the building of gunboats and facilities in which to keep them in readiness for long periods of time. National leaders do not usually display the interest or talent for dealing with such technical problems, but Jefferson was no ordinary leader, according to Johanna Johnston, who describes his interest in building up the navy:

"His inventiveness was stirred to action again. Even a peaceful nation should not allow itself to be so unprepared. Even a peaceful nation should have some sort of war fleet, ready for action in case of emergency. As for the ships being built so hastily, what would become of them when the threat had ended? He remembered how, when he was in Italy, he had seen a system of dry docks in which ships could be kept in a partially finished state for years, ready for swift completion and launching. If the United States had a similar system of dry docks, the ships now being built could be stored safely through the years as insurance against future troubles. He got out his notes on the dry docks in Venice. He studied them and pondered how such dry docks might be revised and adapted for American needs. At last he designed and had built a model of a dry dock which he was sure could easily be erected in the Navy Yard in Washington. The docks in Italy had been kept dry by constant pumping, but Jefferson had contrived to combine a lock [a canal with a system for raising and lowering ships] with a common wet dock to achieve the same result without such labor. In a dock like this, and in similar docks elsewhere, Jefferson proposed to have 'a proper number of vessels always ready to be launched.' . . . A special [congressional] committee was set up to investigate the invention, and reported favorably. But the rest of the Congressmen were not so impressed. They sniffed and sneered and called it 'visionary and impractical.' So Jefferson's dry dock remained a model, one of his inventions he was never able to put to the test."

time, fanciful, and they refused even to consider it seriously. While arguments about defense versus offense continued, the United States remained unprepared for a large-scale war.

Bringing Shipping to a Standstill

Jefferson was convinced that his time was better spent in trying to avoid war than in preparing for it. In keeping with his other pacifist policies, he reacted to the *Chesapeake* incident and other British and French provocations without violence. Jefferson decided to teach both the British and French a lesson. In December 1807, he proposed and Congress passed the Embargo Act, which kept U.S. ships bound for any foreign nation from leaving American ports. The embargo was designed to cut off American trade supplies, such as grain and manufactured goods, from the two warring countries and their other trading partners. This, Jefferson reasoned, would hurt the countries so much economically that they would be forced to come to terms with the United States.

Jefferson was both frustrated and embarrassed when, over the course of the following year, the embargo proved a failure. The British and French were much less dependent on American trade than Jefferson had supposed. And at the same time, the

While the embargo was in effect, needed goods were transported overland in wagons rather than by sea. The embargo proved less successful than Jefferson had hoped.

United States was more dependent on a steady inflow of foreign goods than he had imagined. As a result, American shippers and businesspeople suffered more than their foreign counterparts. While the British continued defiantly to impress American sailors, the U.S. economy suffered. With shipping at a standstill, thousands of U.S. citizens were unemployed. Many farmers could not sell their crops and went bankrupt because their foreign markets had been closed off. A British traveler who visited the normally thriving port of New York described the grim silence that hung over the town:

> The port indeed was full of shipping, but they [the ships] were dismantled and laid up; their decks were cleared, their hatches fastened down, and scarcely a sailor was to be found on board. Not a box, bale, cask, barrel, or package was to be seen upon the wharves. Many of the counting-houses [businesses] were shut up, or advertised to be let [rented out]; and the few solitary merchants, clerks, porters, and laborers that were to be seen were walking about with their hands in their pockets. The coffee-houses were almost empty; the streets, near the water-side, were almost deserted; the grass had begun to grow upon the wharves.[57]

Eventually, Jefferson's embargo did hurt the British economy. But by that time, so many U.S. lawmakers, both Republicans and Federalists, were against the act that Jefferson felt obliged to retreat. In March 1809, as one of his last official acts as president, Jefferson repealed the embargo for all nations except Britain and France.

No Regrets

At the end of his second term, Jefferson, weary of public service, decided not to run again for the presidency. Although he had managed to keep the United States out of war, the peace for which he had struggled so hard was not to last. After he left office, tensions between the United States and Britain continued to mount. Within two years, the war hawks in Congress became a majority. At their insistence, the United States fought the War of 1812 under Jefferson's successor, James Madison. Jefferson later took the view that the war was

The War of 1812 was fought under Jefferson's successor, James Madison. Jefferson had great respect for Madison's intelligence and leadership abilities.

probably inevitable. Because long-standing differences between the two countries had never been resolved, he believed, the war was an unfortunate but necessary continuation of the Revolution. He called the new war "the second weaning from [elimination of] British principles, British attachments, British manners." The United States, he said, would not have had a chance for real prosperity unless, through war, it had ended the "continued subordination [dependence] to the interests and influence of England."[58]

Jefferson felt that as president he had done everything humanly possible to avoid war. He was aware that many of his policies in his second term had been less than successful. Indeed, many of his critics, and even some modern historians, criticized his foreign policy and called him weak. Nevertheless, Jefferson pointed out in his own defense that no American had died as a result of his policies. "I have the consolation to reflect," he said, "that during the period of my administration not a drop of the blood of a single fellow citizen was shed by the sword of war or of the law."[59]

As the last days and hours of his presidency ticked away, Jefferson's excitement mounted. Finally, he would be able to enjoy his long-awaited retirement at the age of sixty-six. He had served his country loyally and diligently in every imaginable capacity. His remaining years now would be his own. He wrote to a friend:

Jefferson did everything possible to avoid another war. Although he succeeded in holding off war during his final term as president, the United States went to war after he left office.

Jefferson and Madison

Jefferson handpicked James Madison to succeed him as president partly because he greatly respected Madison's intelligence and leadership abilities. He also considered Madison one of his closest friends. The casual, good-natured relationship between these two gifted men is illustrated in the following letter from Jefferson to Madison, dated March 13, 1791:

"What say you to taking a peaceful wade into the country at noon? It will be pleasant above head [clear sky] at least, and the party will finish by dining here [at Monticello]. Information that Colonel Beckwith [a British minister neither man liked] is coming to be an inmate [roommate] with you, and I presume not a desirable one, encourages me to make a proposition . . . that is, to come and take a bed and plate with me [stay at my place]. I have four rooms, of which any one is at your service. Three of them are up two pair of stairs, the other on the ground-floor, and can be in readiness to receive you in twenty-four hours. Let me entreat [beg] you . . . to do it, if it be not disagreeable to you. To me it will be a relief from a solitude of which I have too much; and it will . . . not increase my expenses an atom. When I get my library open, you will often find a convenience in being close at hand to it. . . . Let me, I beseech you [ask you urgently], have a favorable answer to both propositions."

Never did a prisoner, released from his chains, feel such relief as I shall on shaking off the shackles of power. Nature intended me for the tranquil pursuits of science, by rendering them my supreme delight. But the enormities of the time in which I have lived, have forced me to take a part in resisting them, and to commit myself to the boisterous [turbulent] ocean of political passions. I thank God for the opportunity of retiring from them.[60]

On the day of Madison's inauguration, Jefferson mounted his horse and rode alone to the Capitol. There, he congratulated Madison and wished him well in his new and difficult job. After spending a few more days packing, Jefferson boarded a carriage and left for Monticello. Soon, he found the roads so rough that he climbed out and continued on horseback. For three days, the sixty-six-year-old statesman rode through a blinding snowstorm, just as he had on his honeymoon journey so many years before. When he finally reached Monticello, he found his daughter, grandchildren, and slaves waiting for him. Happy to see him and proud of his accomplishments, they huddled around him during the walk up the winding road to the house. At last, he was home to stay.

7 Man on a Hilltop

In March 1809, Thomas Jefferson permanently retired to Monticello. During the last seventeen years of his life, he rarely ventured far from his own house and property. To some relatives and friends, it appeared that he was trying to make up for all the years he had missed on his beloved hilltop. Now relieved of the duties of public service, he could fully enjoy the many leisure pursuits and activities that made him most happy.

A Host of Experiments and Inventions

Almost immediately after settling in at Monticello, Jefferson busied himself with a host of projects. Some of these he had begun or tinkered with before. For example, he had experimented with new farming and gardening ideas for years. Now, he expanded these experiments and regularly passed on the results, as well as seeds, clippings, and other samples, to local farmers. Jefferson hoped, in time, to make significant improvements in American plant cultivation and food production. Experimental gardens sprang up all around Monticello. Jefferson raised new strains of rice, and he planted pecans, walnuts, figs from France,

strawberries and corn from Italy, silk trees, and apricots. Jefferson kept track of the progress of every garden, often of every plant, demonstrating an astounding eye for detail. One day, the overseer of the estate removed two or three of the tens of thousands of trees on the property. To his surprise, the retired president immediately noticed they were missing.

While tending to his agricultural projects, Jefferson also spent many hours fine-tuning his inventions. One of his most ingenious devices was a mechanical dumbwaiter, an elevatorlike device. He installed it in the dining room to raise wine bottles and other supplies from the cellar. In addition, Johanna Johnston recounted that Jefferson

> had the moldboard [blade] for his plow cast in iron, as thin as possible. He noted in his Farm Book that it dug a furrow "9 inches wide and 6 inches deep with only two small horses or mules" to draw it. And he added, with satisfaction, that it did beautiful work. Other inventions occurred to him. . . . He experimented with various machines that would manufacture needed goods on a small scale. He had spinning machines set up to manufacture the linen, cotton and wool needed to clothe his

family and servants, and he kept careful notes on their efficiency. . . . Jefferson had always been a tireless letter writer. Now even he grew a little weary under his tremendous load of correspondence. He was glad these days to have the help of another man's invention . . . the polygraph, a writing desk with from two to five pens suspended from a mechanism above it in such a way that any movement made by one pen was exactly duplicated by the others. . . . With its help he could write an original letter and have a duplicate for his files. . . . Jefferson thought of improvements for the

Jefferson found good use for another invention— this one not his own. The polygraph allowed him to make duplicates of his many letters to friends and acquaintances.

polygraph . . . [and] passed [them] on to the inventor who incorporated them into his later models.[61]

The dumbwaiter (below), one of Jefferson's most ingenious inventions, was concealed in a fireplace at Monticello. Jefferson used it to bring wine and other items up from the cellar.

Creating Pathways of Learning

In a sense, Jefferson's greatest invention was Monticello itself, a model of comfort and efficiency for its day. Between 1810 and 1817, he expanded and improved the house once more, making it larger and more attractive than ever. With the same care and diligence lavished on the grounds, he directed the house's design and construction. During these years, he often generously allowed visitors to tour the home, and they marveled at the way he had personally overseen the smallest details. George Ticknor, a young Bostonian who visited Monticello in February 1815, described the house and grounds:

The lawn on the top [of the mountain] was artificially formed by cutting down the peak of the height [hill]. In its center and facing the south east Mr.

Monticello's kitchen, like the rest of the house, was designed to be functional and comfortable.

Jefferson has placed his house, which is of brick, two stories high in the wings, with a piazza [porch] in front of a receding center. You enter by a glass folding-door into a hall. . . . On one side hang the head and horns of an elk, a deer, and a buffalo; another is covered with curiosities which Lewis and Clark found in their wild and perilous expedition. On the third [wall] . . . was the head of a mammoth. . . . On the fourth side, in odd union with a fine painting of the Repentance of Saint Peter, is an Indian map on leather of the southern waters of the Missouri, and an Indian representation of a bloody battle, handed down in their traditions. Through this hall—or rather museum—we passed to the dining room, and sent our letters to Mr. Jefferson, who was of course in his study. Here again we found ourselves surrounded with paintings that seemed good. . . . A large and rather elegant

Entrance doors to most rooms at Monticello were double-sealed to keep sound from traveling and windows often consisted of two panes of glass to keep out the cold.

The Library of Congress

Jefferson established the Library of Congress in 1800 as a place where the president, vice-president, and members of Congress could go to read, study, and borrow books. In 1815, he sold his own book collection of more than six thousand volumes to the library, which already had about the same number. In time, the Library of Congress grew into the largest library in the world. As Johanna Johnston recalls, worries about his debts originally gave Jefferson the idea to sell his books:

"He sat in his library and pondered a question that has occupied a good many people from time to time across the centuries. Where was he going to get the money to pay his debts? . . . He looked around at his books, literally thousands of them, collected over the course of fifty years. There were books on history and physics, astronomy, mathematics, religion . . . think of a subject on which a book might have been written and Jefferson had a book on it. He knew the value of his library and had long since decided that when he died, it should be offered to Congress to buy for the nation at whatever price Congress wanted to set. Now he thought of the fact that in the recent War of 1812 . . . the British had done some grievous damage in Washington. Not only had they burned the Capitol and Executive Mansion, they had also burned the library of books which Congress had begun to collect. Jefferson decided to offer his library to the nation immediately if Congress wished to purchase it. 'Eighteen or twenty wagons,' he wrote, 'would place it in Washington in a single trip. . . .' Congress . . . accepted at once and offered $25,000 for the books. . . . Jefferson breathed a sigh of relief, and paid off $15,000 worth of debts. And immediately began buying books again. So he rescued himself from bankruptcy, and at the same time gave his country a fabulous collection of books which became the nucleus for today's world-famous Library of Congress."

room twenty or thirty feet high, which with the hall I have described composes the whole center of the house from top to bottom. The floor of this room . . . is formed of alternate diamonds of cherry and beech, and kept polished as highly as if it were of fine mahogany. [The] collection of books [in the library], now so much talked about, consists of about seven thousand volumes, contained in a suite of fine rooms; and is arranged in the catalogue and on the shelves according to the divisions and subdivisions of human learning.[62]

Monticello is a testament to Jefferson's inventiveness. He designed the bedrooms with skylights for overhead lighting in the

Jefferson's dream of a publicly funded university became reality when the Virginia Legislature established the University of Virginia in 1819. Jefferson served as its first director.

daytime. He also double-sealed the entrance doors to most rooms to better soundproof them and installed windows with double glass to keep out the cold. Everywhere in the house, there is evidence that Jefferson was constantly tinkering, endlessly experimenting with new ideas.

Indeed, creating the opportunity to learn and experiment in the comforts of home was Jefferson's main objective in designing the house. Though proud and happy to show his home to visitors, he did not intend it to be merely a museum. He wanted others to make full use of Monticello's comforts and devices. So he invited his daughters and grandchildren to live with him. By 1818, twelve grandchildren shared the house and grounds with the former president. The aging but still energetic Jefferson often directed the younger children in footraces on the lawns. He also regularly encouraged them to study hard and explore new ideas. Later, many of them recalled the pleasures of playing and learning in the unique environment their grandfather had carved from that hilltop. According to Jefferson's granddaughter, Virginia Trist:

One of our earliest amusements was in running races on the terrace, or around the lawn. He placed us according to our ages, giving the youngest and smallest the start of all the others by some yards, and so on; and then he raised his arm high, with his white handkerchief in his hand, on which our eager eyes were fixed, and slowly counted three, at which number he dropped the handkerchief, and we started off. . . . Whenever an opportunity occurred, he sent us books; and he never saw a little story or piece of poetry in a newspaper, suited to our ages and tastes, that he did not preserve it and send it to us.[63]

But Jefferson realized that learning outside the home was important, too. For decades, he had proposed and sponsored legislation for educational programs for the nation. As early as 1800, he had called for building a huge, modern university to be supported by public funds. In his retirement, he took upon himself the monumental task of making that institution a reality. Between 1814 and 1816, Jefferson proposed a curriculum for the school, helped find the money to construct it, and even designed its buildings. Virginia's legislature approved the plans and in 1819 established the University of Virginia with Jefferson as rector, the head of the university.

Maintaining and Renewing Old Friendships

Despite all of his projects and activities, Jefferson still kept in constant touch with his friends and former colleagues in Washington. Jefferson's successors, Republican presidents James Madison and James Monroe, often discussed important affairs of state with him and asked him for advice. The most notable example occurred in October 1823. One day, Monroe informed Jefferson of a secret dispatch from Foreign Minister George Canning of Great Britain. The British had evidence that Russia, Prussia, Spain, Austria, and France were planning to launch military expeditions against South America. They wanted to recapture some of the nations there that had recently gained their independence. Canning asked Monroe if the United States

Jefferson and Adams

In their long and fruitful correspondence, Jefferson and his friend John Adams discussed every imaginable subject. Both men were religious but also fascinated by science, and they sometimes tried to explain religious concepts using scientific principles. In this excerpt from Jefferson's August 15, 1820, letter, he comments on Adams's remarks in a previous letter concerning the existence of the human soul:

"Let me turn to your puzzling letter of May 12. on matter, spirit, motion, etc. It's croud [crowd] of scepticisms kept me from my sleep. I read it, and laid it down: read it, and laid it down, again and again. . . . I feel bodies which are not myself: there are other existences then. I call them *matter.* I feel them changing place. This gives me *motion.* Where there is an absence of matter, I call it *void,* or *nothing,* or *immaterial space.* . . . To talk of *immaterial* existences is to talk of *nothings.* To say that the human soul, angels, god, are immaterial, is to say they are *nothings,* or that there is no god, no angels, no soul. . . . At what age of the Christian church this heresy of *immaterialism,* this masked atheism, crept in, I do not know. But a heresy it certainly is. Jesus taught nothing of it. He told us indeed that 'God is a spirit,' but he has not defined what a spirit is, nor said that it is not *matter.* And the antient [ancient] fathers generally, if not universally, held it to be matter: light and thin indeed, and ethereal [heavenly] gas; but still matter."

would be interested in helping the British, who were now on friendly terms with the United States, to thwart the invasion. Monroe wanted Jefferson's advice before giving Canning an answer.

Jefferson told Monroe that the United States should immediately agree to the British offer. Furthermore, U.S. foreign policy should constantly aim to keep European nations from establishing power bases in the Americas. Otherwise, these nations might someday threaten the United States on its own borders. Jefferson wrote Monroe:

> America, North and South, has a set of interests distinct from those of Europe, and peculiarly her own. She should therefore have a system [policy] of her own, separate and apart from Europe. . . . [We should] introduce and establish the American system, of keeping out of our land all foreign powers, of never permitting those of Europe to intermeddle with the affairs of our nations.[64]

Taking Jefferson's advice, Monroe, with the aid of the British, established a "hands-off" policy regarding the Western Hemisphere, a warning to European and other powers to stay out of American affairs. This standing policy became known as the Monroe Doctrine. The United States, however, was not strong enough to enforce the doctrine at the time. But Britain's formidable naval power was enough to discourage any would-be aggressors.

During his retirement, many other former colleagues wrote to Jefferson for advice. Others wanted to share and compare ideas on many subjects with the master of Monticello, and he kept up a lively correspondence, writing and receiving dozens of letters each week. One former colleague whose correspondence Jefferson sorely missed was John Adams. The two revolutionary comrades and Founding Fathers did not speak to each other for many years after the 1800 election. Adams remained bitter over the campaign and election loss, and Jefferson felt slighted by Adams's continued silence.

Finally, in 1812, at the urging of a mutual friend, the two men resumed their friendship. Adams made the first move, choosing not to mention the long years of silence between them. He sent Jefferson a short but cordial letter informing him that

While serving as president of the United States, James Monroe often turned to Jefferson for advice on important matters of state.

In 1812, John Adams (above) and Jefferson renewed their friendship after several years of estrangement. The renewal of this friendship brought both men great pleasure.

he was sending two pieces of homespun cloth to Monticello. "All of my Family whom you formerly knew are well," Adams added. In his reply, Jefferson thanked Adams and proceeded to describe domestic manufacturing in Virginia. Jefferson closed the letter by saying, "No circumstances have ... suspended for one moment my sincere esteem for you; and I now salute you with unchanged affections and respect." Thus began one of the greatest examples of sustained correspondence in American political history.

Over the years, the two former presidents discussed numerous subjects, ranging from agriculture and natural history to politics and philosophy. Each offered advice without being asked and kept the other informed about old friends and current rumors from Washington. They also became an increasing comfort to each other as they grew older, often confiding their most personal feelings. This was the case when a distraught Adams wrote on October 20, 1815, that his wife, Abigail, was extremely ill:

> The dear Partner of my Life for fifty four Years as a Wife and for many Years more as a Lover, now lyes in extremis [deathly ill], forbidden [by doctors] to speak or be spoken to. If human Life is a Bubble [meaningless], no matter how soon it breaks. If it is as I firmly believe an immortal Existence We ought patiently to wait the Instructions of the great Teacher. I am, Sir, your deeply afflicted Friend.

Abigail Adams died of typhoid fever eight days later. On November 13, Jefferson wrote to Adams:

> The public papers, my dear friend, announce the fatal event of which your letter of Oct. 20. had given me ominous foreboding [fear and worry]. . . . I know well, and feel what you have lost, what you have suffered, are suffering, and have yet to endure. The same trials have taught me that, for ills so immeasurable, time and silence are the only medicines. . . . It is of some comfort to us both that the term is not very distant at which we are . . . to ascend in essence [as spirits] to an ecstatic [joyful] meeting with the friends we have loved and lost and whom we shall still love and never lose again. God bless you and support you under your heavy affliction.[65]

Two Great Lives End Together

The renewal of his friendship with Adams pleased Jefferson greatly. There was one old friend, however, whom Jefferson had not seen since 1789 and whom he deeply missed—the Marquis de Lafayette. The two had periodically corresponded by letter, but by 1824, Jefferson had given up hope of ever actually seeing his French comrade again. Then came the news that President Monroe had invited Lafayette to visit the United States. Jefferson's excitement increased for months until the day in November 1824 when Lafayette's carriage

Jefferson longed to see his old friend Lafayette again. He got his wish in 1824, when the French general visited America at President James Monroe's request. It was a joyous and emotional reunion for both Jefferson and Lafayette.

rolled up the winding road to Monticello. A crowd had gathered to witness the meeting. Jefferson's grandson Jefferson Randolph remembered how, upon seeing Lafayette, the eighty-two-year-old Jefferson "got into a shuffling, quickened gait until they threw themselves with tears into each other's arms." According to Randolph, "Of the 3 or 400 persons present not a sound escaped except an occasional supprest sob, there was not a dry eye in the crowd."[66] Lafayette's six-week visit to Monticello was one of the highlights of Jefferson's later life. The two reminisced about old times and also discussed current events, about which they both had strong opinions.

After Lafayette's return to France, Jefferson stayed busy, but his health steadily deteriorated. By the spring of 1825, he was so weak that often he could neither walk nor stand, and he spent much of his time reclining on his couch. Yet, though his body had grown feeble, his mind remained bright and alert. He still wrote and received many letters, corresponding with Lafayette alone some one hundred more times.

But by late June 1826, Jefferson was too weak even to write letters. Confined to his bed, he realized that he was dying, but he wanted desperately to hold on a few more days until July 4, the fiftieth anniversary of the Declaration of Independence and the birth of the United States. At seven o'clock in the evening on July 3, in a barely audible voice, Jefferson asked his doctor if it was July 4 yet, and the doctor answered that it soon would be. Jefferson Randolph, who stood by with other relatives, later recalled his grandfather's final hours:

> As twelve o'clock at night approached, we anxiously desired that his death

An Emotional Reunion

One of the most emotional moments of Jefferson's life occurred in 1824, when his old friend Lafayette, the French statesman, arrived at Monticello for a visit. The two had not seen each other for thirty-five years. Fawn Brodie describes the circumstances of Lafayette's visit:

"When Lafayette at age sixty-seven was invited by President James Monroe to visit America, he was 100,000 francs in debt. Nevertheless, he borrowed the money for his passage, and planned an elaborate itinerary [schedule] in the New World. Although he spent only one day in Quincy, Massachusetts, with John Adams, he stayed almost six weeks with Jefferson, and later on his way home returned again to see him. In November 1824 a great crowd assembled at Monticello to witness the first meeting of Lafayette and Jefferson, who had not seen each other since 1789, shortly after the fall of the Bastille [a French prison attacked by mobs during the French Revolution]. Jefferson Randolph, who helped with the celebration, described how his grandfather [Jefferson], feeble with age, walked down from his terrace as Lafayette descended from his carriage. Jefferson, he said, 'got into a shuffling, quickened gait until they threw themselves with tears into each other's arms—of the 3 or 400 persons present not a sound escaped except an occasional supprest sob, there was not a dry eye in the crowd—altho invited into the house none would enter [out of respect for the privacy of the two men].' Later there was a formal dinner in the still unfinished Rotunda of the University of Virginia, with . . . the best French wine from the Monticello cellar."

should be hallowed [made sacred] by the Anniversary of Independence. At fifteen minutes before twelve we stood noting the minute-hand of the watch, hoping for a few minutes of prolonged life. At four A.M. he called the servants in attendance with a strong and clear voice. . . . He did not speak again. . . . About eleven . . . fixing his eyes upon me, and moving his lips, I applied a wet sponge to his mouth, which he sucked and appeared to relish—this was the last evidence he gave of consciousness. He ceased to breathe, without a struggle, fifty minutes past meridian [noon]— July 4, 1826. I closed his eyes with my own hands.[67]

The Declaration's Lasting Significance

In old age, Jefferson summed up the importance of the Declaration in 1826, when he was invited to Washington for the celebration of the fiftieth anniversary of the document and of the birth of the United States. Only days before his death at age eighty-three, Jefferson said of the Declaration:

"May it be to the world what I believe it will be, the signal of arousing men to burst the chains under which monkish ignorance and superstition had persuaded them to bind themselves, and to assume the blessings and security of self-government. That form [of government] which we have substituted, restores the free right to the unbounded exercise of reason and freedom of opinion. All eyes [around the world] are opened, or opening, to the rights of man. The general spread of the light of science has already laid open to every view the palpable [obvious] truth that the mass of mankind has not been born with saddles on their backs, nor a favored few booted and spurred, ready to ride them legitimately by the grace of God. These are grounds for hope for others. For ourselves let the annual return of this day forever refresh our recollections of these rights, and an undiminished devotion to them."

As they mourned Jefferson, Randolph and the others had no way of knowing that one of history's greatest coincidences was happening. That same day, Jefferson's friend John Adams also lay dying in faraway Quincy, Massachusetts. Adams, too, had succeeded in hanging on to life until the special day that held so much meaning for them both. Unaware of his comrade's passing, at the moment of death, Adams offered some last reassuring words for the nation: "Thomas Jefferson still survives."

Jefferson's Legacy Endures

It has been said that great men and women achieve a kind of immortality through the works they leave behind for the benefit of future generations. Few human beings have left a legacy as large and as rich as that of Thomas Jefferson. He survives because his ideas and deeds made an unforgettable

Jefferson's ideas and deeds profoundly shaped America. His life and actions left a deep and lasting imprint on the nation he helped to form.

imprint not only on his own times but on future ages as well.

Jefferson's tireless devotion to serving his country profoundly shaped the events of half a century of American life. In addition to helping establish the country and mold its ideals, he doubled its size and opened the way for its future expansion and development. As Nathan Schachner put it, "His long life spanned the birth and establishment of a new nation, and no man contributed more to both than he did."

Yet Jefferson was more than a patriot and political leader. His unique character and versatility made him a legend in his own time. "In an era of complex and many-sided men," said Schachner, "he was without doubt the most complex and many-sided of them all. He literally took all knowledge to be his province, and his insatiable curiosity and probing intellect took him along amazing highways and byways. In all he did supremely well." Jefferson's contemporaries recognized his genius and referred to him in his retirement as the "sage of Monticello." The man who dwelled on a remote Virginia hilltop became a living symbol of the country itself and of the progress that could be achieved through knowledge. The key to a better future, Jefferson believed, was the human mind constantly perfecting itself through learning. "He profoundly believed in the perfectability of mankind," said Schachner, "and foresaw an endless vista of upward and onward progress."[68]

The extraordinary respect Jefferson's contemporaries had for him, his accomplishments, and his vision for the nation is evident in the following remarks by Judge Dabney Carr of the Virginia Court of Appeals. Shortly after Jefferson's death, Carr wrote what might stand as a fitting epitaph for Jefferson:

> The loss of Mr. Jefferson is one over which the whole world will mourn. He was one of those ornaments and benefactors of the human race whose death forms an epoch [end of an era] and creates a sensation throughout the whole circle of civilized man. . . . Taken as a whole, history presents nothing so grand, so beautiful, so peculiarly felicitous [agreeable] in all the great points, as the life and character of Thomas Jefferson.[69]

After his death, Jefferson's influence on the nation remained just as profound. So important were his contributions to the government and philosophy of the United States that every generation of Americans since has felt their impact. And every generation to come will also feel it. According to Pulitzer Prize-winning historian Leonard Levy, this is because Jefferson's ideas about human equality and freedom are embodied in the unique laws and institutions of the United States. They are part of what make the nation strong and flexible. They are part of why Americans wake up each day under a government run by their own representatives rather than by a dictator. As long as the nation survives, Jefferson will live on in its laws and institutions. Said Levy:

> Jefferson "still survives," to quote the famous deathbed words of John Adams, because a free people still cherishes the spirit of liberty and its foremost exponent among the founders of the Republic. Jefferson hated tyranny and war, poverty and privilege, bigotry and ignorance; he hated whatever crippled man's spirit or body. His influence was zealously devoted to securing the conditions of freedom that would make possible the "pursuit of happiness" by all. He championed free public education and attacked the aristocratic system. . . . He condemned slavery and recommended its gradual abolition. He saved untold thousands from bondage by championing the end of the foreign slave trade. . . . He advocated freedom of the press and resisted the noxious [disgusting] Alien and Sedition Acts. . . . His legacy was the idea that . . . the state must be bitted and bridled [guided] by a bill of rights which should be construed in the most generous terms, its protections not to be the playthings of momentary majorities or of those in power.[70]

Jefferson did not consider himself a great man. He found the increasing adulation and hero worship he experienced late in his life perplexing. He kept insisting that he was just a simple man who worked hard and used his time wisely. Similarly, he did not foresee the greatness he would achieve after his death. His unusual mental gifts, versatility, energy, and dedication to duty all seemed so natural to him that he did not understand the true significance of many of his accomplishments. He

The Jefferson Memorial in Washington, D.C. is inscribed with Jefferson's own words, proclaiming his enduring passion for freedom of human spirit and thought.

wished to be remembered for only a few and quite specific achievements. He requested that the following words be engraved on his tombstone:

> Here was buried
> Thomas Jefferson
> Author of the
> Declaration of Independence
> of the Statute of Virginia for
> Religious Freedom
> & Father of the University of Virginia

Although these and his other deeds will always be considered important, perhaps Jefferson's greatest legacy stems from what motivated the deeds. He possessed a restless, defiant spirit that refused to accept the suppression of free thought and expression. This rebellious spirit, Leonard Levy pointed out, infected others around him and continues to inspire people today. And it is through that spirit, more than anything else, that Thomas Jefferson survives. Levy claimed, "The words chosen for inscription on the Jefferson Memorial [in Washington, D.C.]: 'I have sworn on the altar of God, eternal hostility against every form of tyranny over the mind of man,' reflect his enduring spirit and will speak to mankind as long as liberty is cherished on earth."[71]

Notes

Introduction: A Mind That Asked Why

1. Quoted in Roger Bruns, *Thomas Jefferson*. New York: Chelsea House, 1986.

2. Bruns, *Thomas Jefferson*.

3. Johanna Johnston, *Thomas Jefferson: His Many Talents*. New York: Dodd, Mead, 1961.

Chapter 1: "A Thirst for Knowledge"

4. Quoted in Leonard Wibberley, *Young Man from the Piedmont: The Youth of Thomas Jefferson*. New York: Ariel Books, 1963.

5. Wibberley, *Young Man from the Piedmont*.

6. Letter to William Wirt, quoted in Claude G. Bowers, *The Young Jefferson: 1743–1789*. Boston: Houghton Mifflin, 1945.

7. Vincent Sheean, *Thomas Jefferson: Father of Democracy*. New York: Random House, 1953.

8. Letter to John Adams, October 28, 1813, quoted in Lester J. Cappon, ed., *The Adams-Jefferson Letters*. Chapel Hill: University of North Carolina Press, 1959.

9. Letter to Edward Bancroft, quoted in Fawn M. Brodie, *Thomas Jefferson: An Intimate History*. New York: W. W. Norton, 1974.

10. Quoted in Merrill D. Peterson, *Thomas Jefferson and the New Nation*. New York: Oxford University Press, 1970.

11. Letter to T. J. Randolph, quoted in Sarah N. Randolph, ed., *The Domestic Life of Thomas Jefferson*. New York: Harper, 1871. Reprinted in Charlottesville: University Press of Virginia, 1978.

12. Bruns, *Thomas Jefferson*.

13. Sheean, *Thomas Jefferson: Father of Democracy*.

14. Quoted in Wibberley, *Young Man from the Piedmont*.

Chapter 2: "Rebellion in the Wind"

15. From the Declaration of Independence.

16. Quoted in Brodie, *Thomas Jefferson: An Intimate History*.

17. Peterson, *Thomas Jefferson and the New Nation*.

18. Quoted in Peterson, *Thomas Jefferson and the New Nation*.

19. Randolph, *The Domestic Life of Thomas Jefferson*.

20. Quoted in Sarah N. Randolph, *The Domestic Life of Thomas Jefferson*.

21. Sheean, *Thomas Jefferson: Father of Democracy*.

Chapter 3: "Architect of Freedom"

22. From the Declaration of Independence.

23. Quoted in Henry S. Randall, *The Life of Thomas Jefferson*. New York: Derby & Jackson, 1858.

24. Quoted in Nathan Schachner, *Thomas Jefferson: A Biography*. New York: Thomas Yoseloff, 1957.

25. Quoted in Schachner, *Thomas Jefferson: A Biography*.

26. From *Autobiography*, in Adrienne Koch and William Peden, eds., *Life and Selected Writings of Thomas Jefferson*. New York: Random House, 1944.

27. Irwin Unger, *These United States: The Questions of Our Past.* Boston: Little, Brown, 1978.

28. Quoted in Bruns, *Thomas Jefferson.*

29. From *Notes on the State of Virginia,* in *Thomas Jefferson: Writings.* Compiled by Merrill D. Peterson. Washington, DC: Library of America, 1984.

30. Quoted in Koch and Peden, *Life and Selected Writings of Thomas Jefferson.*

Chapter 4: "The Reluctant Diplomat"

31. Quoted in Bruns, *Thomas Jefferson.*

32. Schachner, *Thomas Jefferson: A Biography.*

33. From *Notes on the State of Virginia,* in *Thomas Jefferson: Writings.*

34. Quoted in Henry Moscow, *Thomas Jefferson and His World.* New York: American Heritage Publishing, 1960.

35. Quoted in Moscow, *Thomas Jefferson and His World.*

36. Moscow, *Thomas Jefferson and His World.*

37. Quoted in Francis W. Hirst, *Life and Letters of Thomas Jefferson.* New York: Macmillan, 1926.

38. Moscow, *Thomas Jefferson and His World.*

39. Bruns, *Thomas Jefferson.*

Chapter 5: "Reaching for New Horizons"

40. Quoted in Peterson, *Thomas Jefferson and the New Nation.*

41. Quoted in Schachner, *Thomas Jefferson: A Biography.*

42. From *First Inaugural Address,* in Koch and Peden, *Life and Selected Writings of Thomas Jefferson.*

43. Quoted in Peterson, *Thomas Jefferson and the New Nation.*

44. Unger, *These United States.*

45. Brodie, *Thomas Jefferson: An Intimate History.*

46. Virginius Dabney, *The Jefferson Scandals: A Rebuttal.* New York: Dodd, Mead, 1981.

47. Peterson, *Thomas Jefferson and the New Nation.*

48. James Truslow Adams, *The Living Jefferson.* New York: Charles Scribner's Sons, 1936.

49. Quoted in Schachner, *Thomas Jefferson: A Biography.*

50. Quoted in Hirst, *Life and Letters of Thomas Jefferson.*

51. Quoted in Peterson, *Thomas Jefferson and the New Nation.*

52. Quoted in Peterson, *Thomas Jefferson and the New Nation.*

Chapter 6: "Struggle for Peace"

53. Quoted in Bruns, *Thomas Jefferson.*

54. Merrill D. Peterson, "Thomas Jefferson: A Brief Life," in Lally Weymouth, ed., *Thomas Jefferson: The Man, His World, His Influence.* London: Weidenfeld & Nicolson, 1973.

55. Unger, *These United States.*

56. Quoted in Schachner, *Thomas Jefferson: A Biography.*

57. From *Lambert's Travels,* quoted in Schachner, *Thomas Jefferson: A Biography.*

58. Quoted in Peterson, *Thomas Jefferson and the New Nation.*

59. Quoted in Moscow, *Thomas Jefferson and His World.*

60. Quoted in Peterson, *Thomas Jefferson and the New Nation.*

Chapter 7: "Man on a Hilltop"

61. Johnston, *Thomas Jefferson: His Many Talents.*

62. Quoted in Hirst, *Life and Letters of Thomas Jefferson.*

63. Letter of May 26, 1839, quoted in Sarah N. Randolph, *The Domestic Life of Thomas Jefferson.*

64. Letter to James Monroe, October 24, 1823, quoted in Koch and Peden, *Life and Selected Writings of Thomas Jefferson.*

65. Letters quoted: Adams to Jefferson, January 1, 1812; Jefferson to Adams, January 21, 1812; Adams to Jefferson, October 20, 1815; Jefferson to Adams, November 13, 1815, all in Cappon, *The Adams-Jefferson Letters.*

66. Quoted in Brodie, *Thomas Jefferson: An Intimate History.*

67. Jefferson Randolph, quoted in Sarah N. Randolph, *The Domestic Life of Thomas Jefferson.*

Epilogue: "Jefferson's Legacy Endures"

68. Schachner, *Thomas Jefferson: A Biography.*

69. Quoted in Sarah N. Randolph, *The Domestic Life of Thomas Jefferson.*

70. Leonard Levy, "Jefferson as a Civil Libertarian," in Weymouth, *Thomas Jefferson: The Man, His World, His Influence.*

71. Levy, "Jefferson as a Civil Libertarian." Quoted in Weymouth, *Thomas Jefferson: The Man, His World, His Influence.*

For Further Reading

Natalie S. Bober, *Thomas Jefferson: Man on a Mountain*. New York: Atheneum, 1988. A highly descriptive account of Jefferson's life and contributions, written for ambitious and advanced readers.

Roger Bruns, *Thomas Jefferson*. New York: Chelsea House, 1986. A short but lively and clearly written version of Jefferson's life and deeds. Contains many interesting pictures and illustrations.

Johanna Johnston, *Thomas Jefferson: His Many Talents*. New York: Dodd, Mead, 1961. Written for intermediate readers, this volume focuses on Jefferson's varied talents rather than providing a chronological telling of his life. Included are chapters on his endeavors as architect, naturalist, inventor, explorer, and so on.

Manuel Komroff, *Thomas Jefferson*. Lakeville, CT: Grey Castle Books, 1991. A good general account of Jefferson's life and achievements, aimed specifically at young readers.

Milton Meltzer, *Thomas Jefferson: The Revolutionary Aristocrat*. New York: Franklin Watts, 1991. Touches on the main events of Jefferson's life and his important ideas and writings, with a recurring emphasis on the irony that Jefferson was born into the Virginia aristocracy but fought for the rights of the common people.

Henry Moscow, in consultation with Dumas Malone, *Thomas Jefferson and His World*. New York: American Heritage Publishing, 1960. Episodic but very readable account of Jefferson's life and times for intermediate and advanced readers. It is well illustrated.

Leonard Wibberley, *Young Man from the Piedmont: The Youth of Thomas Jefferson*. New York: Ariel Books, 1963. Colorful, well-written book that focuses on the events of Jefferson's life from his birth in 1743 until the Declaration of Independence in 1776.

Works Consulted

Fawn M. Brodie, *Thomas Jefferson: An Intimate History.* New York: W. W. Norton, 1974. Highly detailed and revealing biography of Jefferson that has been criticized for taking the controversial view that Jefferson had a black slave mistress and knowingly allowed one of his children by her to be sold. Regardless of the controversy, Brodie finds and presents fascinating angles that other authors often miss or ignore.

Stuart G. Brown, *Thomas Jefferson.* New York: Washington Square Press, 1963. General view of Jefferson's life and contributions, divided into two sections. The first discusses his life and ideas, and the second discusses the philosophers who influenced him.

Lester J. Cappon, ed., *The Adams-Jefferson Letters.* Chapel Hill: University of North Carolina Press, 1959. The fascinating and revealing correspondence between two of the country's most important Founding Fathers.

Donald Barr Chidsey, *Louisiana Purchase: The Story of the Biggest Real Estate Deal in History.* New York: Crown, 1972. Good general account of Jefferson's purchase of Louisiana, which doubled the size of the United States.

Gilbert Chinard, *Thomas Jefferson: The Apostle of Americanism.* Ann Arbor: University of Michigan Press, 1966. Scholarly work that emphasizes Jefferson's contributions to the formation of American and democratic thought and values.

Virginius Dabney, *The Jefferson Scandals: A Rebuttal.* New York: Dodd, Mead, 1981. Takes exception to the view put forward by Fawn Brodie and other historians that Jefferson had a slave mistress. According to Dabney, this theory is based on false accusations made about Jefferson by a bitter contemporary.

Clara Ingram Judson, *Thomas Jefferson.* Chicago: Follet Publishing, 1952. A thoughtful and concise biography covering the main events of Jefferson's life.

Library of America, *Thomas Jefferson: Writings.* Washington, DC: Library of America, 1984. Collection of Jefferson's works, including the *Autobiography, A Summary View of the Rights of British America, Notes on the State of Virginia,* public papers, addresses, and some letters.

Dumas Malone, *Jefferson the President: First Term 1801–1805.* Boston: Little, Brown, 1970; *Jefferson the President: Second Term, 1805–1809.* Boston: Little, Brown, 1974. Both books are very scholarly and detailed works by one of America's greatest historians and contain many quotes by Jefferson and his contemporaries.

Merrill D. Peterson, *Thomas Jefferson and the New Nation.* New York: Oxford University Press, 1970. Long, well-researched chronicle of Jefferson and his presidency.

Sarah N. Randolph, ed., *The Domestic Life of Thomas Jefferson*. Charlottesville: University Press of Virginia, 1978. Edited by Jefferson's great-granddaughter. A fascinating collection of Jefferson's family letters, including those between him and his children and grandchildren.

Nathan Schachner, *Thomas Jefferson: A Biography*. New York: Thomas Yoseloff, 1957. Detailed, very well written general account of Jefferson's life and presidency. Takes the view that Jefferson was the most complex and versatile man of his time.

Reginald C. Stuart, *The Half-way Pacifist: Thomas Jefferson's View of War*. Toronto: University of Toronto Press, 1978. A brief but interesting exploration of Jefferson's war views. Takes the position that Jefferson hated the idea of war but placed the survival of his country above his personal feelings.

Lally Weymouth, ed., *Thomas Jefferson: The Man, His World, His Influence*. London: Weidenfeld & Nicolson, 1973. Collection of essays by leading historians, each covering a different aspect of Jefferson's character and endeavors. Contains many excellent pictures and illustrations.

Index

Picture Credits

Cover photo by Historical Pictures/Stock Montage

AP/Wide World Photos, 29, 97

The Bettmann Archive, 9, 23(top), 49(bottom), 61, 63, 65(bottom), 70(top), 71(top), 88

Colonial Williamsburg Foundation, 19, 21(both)

Dover Pictorial Archive Series, Dover Publications, Inc., 16(bottom right), 27(both), 42, 43, 55(top)

Historical Pictures/Stock Montage, 12, 44, 57(top)

Library of Congress, 14(top), 16(top and bottom left), 24, 25, 26 (both), 28, 30(both), 32, 34, 39, 40, 46, 49 (top), 50, 51(both), 52, 54, 55(bottom), 57(bottom), 59(top), 73, 81, 82, 90, 91

Monticello, Thomas Jefferson Memorial Foundation, 10, 85(both), 86(both)

National Archives, 59(bottom), 95

Northwind Picture Archives, 14(bottom), 15, 17, 35, 36, 58, 65(top), 70(bottom), 71(middle and bottom), 76, 77, 78, 80, 92

About the Author

Don Nardo is an actor, film director, and composer, as well as an award-winning writer. As an actor, he has appeared in more than fifty stage productions. He has also worked before or behind the camera in twenty films. Several of his musical compositions, including a young person's version of *The War of the Worlds* and the oratorio *Richard III,* have been played by regional orchestras. Mr. Nardo's writing credits include short stories, articles, and more than thirty-five books, including *Lasers, Germs, Gravity, Anxiety and Phobias, The Irish Potato Famine, Exercise, Recycling, The Indian Wars, H. G. Wells,* and *Charles Darwin.* Among his other writings are an episode of ABC's "Spenser: For Hire" and numerous screenplays. Mr. Nardo lives with his wife, Christine, on Cape Cod, Massachusetts.